SUFFERING & DEATH:

The Saint's Highest Calling

by Henry R. Pike

SUFFERING & DEATH:
THE SAINT'S HIGHEST CALLING

International Copyright © 1994
by
EVANGELISTIC LITERATURE ENTERPRISE LTD
(A.C.N. 010 973 976)
P.O. Box 5010, Brendale, 4500
Queensland, Australia
Phone: (07) 205-7100 Fax: (07) 205-7703

First edition printed in Australia 1994
All subsequent editions printed in the United States of America

Second edition revised and enlarged printed in 1994

Third edition printed in 1995

Fourth edition printed in 1997

Fifth edition revised, enlarged and printed in 2002

Sixth edition revised and printed in 2003

ISBN 0 949047 32 5

Contents

Testimony of Charles H. Spurgeon

I bear my willing witness that I owe more to the fire, and the hammer, and the file, than to anything else in my Lord's workshop. I sometimes question whether I have ever learned anything except through the rod. When my schoolroom is darkened, I see most.

Author's Preface

A respected elderly friend once shared with me his personal philosophy of life and death: "We spend about the first thirty years of life making a mess out of mostly everything in general. The next thirty are consumed honestly trying to make amends and put right the heartaches, misdeeds and idiocies of the past. Just about the time we think it's all in order and we can now live life honorably, we glance out the window. Behold, there stands the undertaker by his hearse beckoning us to come with him! It is time to die. With him we must go. Alas! what of my life? I did not live it."

Despite the curious irony in these words, they ring of uncanny truth and experience. Oddly, it seems to happen to most of us this way. Nothing living in the whole of God's vast creation appears to escape blunders, suffering and death. Considering such things, the apostle Paul wrote: "For we know that the whole creation groaneth and travaileth in pain together until now. And not only they, but ourselves also" (Rom. 8:22-23). Everything passes through the "pain machine." Does it all end here?

We are born into this world "crying" and we leave it "sighing." Most of the book of Ecclesiastes was written about the "vanity of life under the sun." Its utter futility and emptiness. Those who know only the "vanity" side of life's fierce odyssey are the hopeless masses struggling in darkness. But the story does not end here. Even the clouds of Ecclesiastes have silver linings. Life can be better than a "hell on earth" and more fulfilling than a "day at the amusement park."

Human life is from Almighty God (Acts 17:24-25). Even the best evolutionist is at his wits' end trying to determine the "source" of his first or original spark of life. The Son of God left Heaven and, in some incredible and indescribable manner, stopped over for nine months in the womb of a virgin named Mary (Lk 1:26-38). Here He clothed Himself with human flesh and was born among mankind. Through this fantastic process, He entered into this thing we call human life. Some thirty years later, having never committed one sin, He died on the cross for the sins of Adam's fallen race. Victoriously, He broke the chains of death, the fetters of the grave and rose triumphant over both. Now, seated at God's right hand in Heaven, He offers to all who will repent and believe the reality of salvation, forgiveness of all sins, eternal sure hope and a new life amid this old one of suffering and tears. However, the pages of the Holy Bible thunder with another, less palatable, reality: this wonderful new life in Christ will include manifold sufferings and, finally, physical death. This truth is not often preached.

There is indeed a sound, rational and biblical theology of suffering and death. This book discusses some of these facts in a practical, even a brutally honest and straight-forward manner. In so doing it is impossible not to mention the healing cults and various abominations operating within this sphere. In touching on these realities I have tried to write in the highest of Christian candor without "having an axe to grind" against any man or movement. At the same time, I have determined to call a "spade a spade and a shovel a shovel," and not white-wash any ploy or plot of the Devil. It is my understanding that our gracious Lord followed the same rule. Thus, the "brutally honest and straight-forward" language interspersed through portions of this book. It is used in writing not only of the sects and cults flourishing on the ignorance, sufferings and sicknesses of humanity, but also in speaking of my own sufferings, doubts and fears as well as those of thousands of other fellow Christians. Within the orbit of hurting and pain we all share a frightful affinity.

All critics of these pages should remember that I have not ventured into deep theological or exegetical explanations of the differences between sufferings, temptations, trials and persecutions. This has not been my intention. One factor looms like a dark storm cloud over this whole issue: if the sufferings, temptations, trials and persecutions of this life are not handled correctly and especially the tormenting problem of unanswered prayer, any or all of them carry the potential of destroying our witness and faith in the Lord Jesus Christ. By destroy, I do not mean losing our soul's salvation. Personally, in the light of the doctrine of justification by faith, I understand this to be impossible. Rather, I mean being plunged into the lamentable condition so graphically described in II Peter 1:8-11. Untold thousands of God's children are presently sinking and drowning in this horrible nightmare of frustration. They soon become barren, unfruitful and blind. The shores of Christianity are strewn with innumerable such shipwrecks.

I have attempted to build this treatise from hundreds of relevant Scriptures (repeating only a few of them) and some of my life's experiences. My chief goal has been to show the children of God, that the cardinal duties and service we are honored to perform for the Master are: "Suffering and Death: The Saint's Highest Calling."

The author, Henry R. Pike, Ph. D.
Johannesburg, South Africa, 1992

Important Notice to Readers

Some will lightly skim through this book, only selecting those portions that are of particular and personal interest. The profitable way to travel over these pages is with your Bible in hand, conscientiously studying each verse listed. Every Scripture is connected with its paragraph or even the immediate sentence being read. All quotes are given to confirm or illuminate the subject under discussion. However, this method of reading does not always make for swift sailing. In such cases you might remember that it is written: "Surely the churning of milk bringeth forth butter . . ." (Prov. 30:33). Therefore, use your Bible and "churn" through these lines. It will give you heavenly butter, and it's cholesterol free!

Lastly, all repetitions are designed to stress a particular point and not bore the reader. Kindly bear with them. Thank you.

The publisher wishes to add that we have labored to produce a book free of typographical and mechanical error. Should we have failed, please be gracious. We follow One who is perfect but we ourselves fall far short of that achievement.

Dedication

These chapters are admiringly dedicated
to faithful Addien,
". . . my companion in tribulation, and in
the kingdom and patience of Jesus Christ"
(Rev. 1:9). She has suffered with me through
it all and loved me more than any mortal in
this world. The best is yet to come when
heaven will be ours *together* with Jesus,
for ever.

Acknowledgements

Sincere thanks to Denis and Joyce Hands,
Elizabeth Blake, Missionary Sidney Hunter,(now in heaven)
and Heather Hodgkinson. Phillip, my youngest son and Patrick
Collard are responsible for the unique computer layouts and
beautiful cover design. My daughter Rosemary and daughter-in-
law Sandra have been of great help. David, my oldest son, was
the unsung hero in the drama that started with Timothy's
leukemia in Sept.1989. He had the *perfect* match and gave the
bone marrow that saved his brother's life. Evangelist Ed Ballew
provided the ticket money for David to fly to Africa for the
operation. (That's how God does these things.) Thanks to all of
you for what you did to make this testimony possible. That great
Bible teacher, Tony Fowler, and his wife Daisy, along with Pastor
Ed Parton and Dr. Keith Purser have opened the door to place this
little book into the hands of hundreds of people.
Lastly, I thank my son Timothy, for it was while praying beside
his hospital bed at Johannesburg, South Africa, in 1990, that God
laid it on my heart to write this true story.

Introduction

You are going now, said they, to the paradise of God wherein you shall see the tree of life, and eat of the never-fading fruit thereof: and when you come there you shall have white robes given you, and your walk and talk shall be every day with the King, even all the days of eternity. There you shall not see again such things as you saw when you were in the lower region upon the earth; to wit, sorrow, sickness, affliction, and death.

From *The Pilgrim's Progress*

The pages you are about to read have been penned not in ink, but in the tears of a servant of God. They are the words not of one who pontificates in the comfortable shelter of a theological ivory tower, but of one who has come to Pauline grips with the reality of authentic Christian servanthood. They are the words of experience, forged between the relentless hammer and anvil of a life lived uncompromisingly for Christ. And out of the ashes of seeming flesh-and-blood defeat, there rises up a Divine anthem of victory. It is the victory of that One of Whom Job, in the depths of his despair, triumphantly declared: "I know that my redeemer liveth."

Dr. Henry Randall Pike is an old-fashioned fundamentalist, a missionary pastor of 40 years' standing, and a man of extraordinary tenderness and painstaking politeness. He is also a two-fisted, no-nonsense giant of Gospel exposition behind a pulpit. The tragic irony is that Dr. Pike is completely paralyzed in both legs. He would be lost without his crutches and the constant support of his precious wife, Addien. To preach, he must clamp himself into a standing position by means of leg-irons. Yet, there was a time in his life when he had the world quite literally at his feet: at the age of 18, he stood on the brink of American football stardom. Then, as these pages so movingly relate, God tackled him. In recent years, Dr. Pike has had the use of only one kidney and, as I write these words on the first day of this new year 1992, he is presently bed ridden in the process of recuperating from serious surgery aimed at preserving the remaining kidney. But this is only part of the story, as the reader will discover. One thing is sure: the author is well-qualified to write on the subject of suffering.

The belief, widely held among many professedly Christian groupings, that conversion comes with an automatic entitlement to health, wealth and prosperity is supported neither by the Bible nor by the second best-selling book in the world, Bunyan's The Pilgrim's Progress. At the end of their journey, Christian and Hopeful would most assuredly have agreed with the theme developed so convincingly by Dr. Pike: that it is the Christian's calling, or vocare, to suffer. I can already hear the howls of condemnation from the know-alls who shout the odds in auditoriums in which the reverential worship of a holy God has been replaced by the happy-clap cacophony of "quick-fix Christianity." They neither understand, nor attempt to explain to their followers, the sublime irony of Christian service: that the abundant life of John 10:10 is inextricable from the tribulation of John 16:33. It is an irony that was precisely understood by Paul as he wrote to the Philippians from a prison cell: "I know both how to be abased, and I know how to abound: every where and in all things I am instructed both to be full and to be hungry, both to abound and to suffer need" (Phil. 4:12). One of the great hymns of Christian assurance does not say: "We have cotton-wool that coddles the soul." No, it says: "We have an ANCHOR that keeps the soul." Dear reader, it is this anchor, and this anchor alone, that has kept the author through his own "storms of life."

I have had the profound privilege of reading these pages in manuscript form and of advising the writer on such mundane matters as grammar and usage. None of the amendments I have suggested, however, can add a jot or tittle of value to the treasure chest of Christian wisdom unlocked here for the benefit of all genuinely born-again saints who would worthily follow in the footsteps of the Master. As you traverse these pages, you will come across the author sharing the Gospel of salvation with terminally ill patients in a Johannesburg, South Africa, cancer ward. The extraordinary element of the situation is that his own son is occupying one of the beds. Here is a picture of a true servant of Christ rising above overwhelming personal anguish to press toward the mark of his high calling.

Some 10 years ago I stood at the front door of a home in the South African town of Alberton, south-east of Johannesburg. As a favor to a third party, I had agreed to deliver a package to the home, which happened to be near my own. My mission completed, I left . . . with a salvation tract in my hand. Some months later, in the study of that very same home, I accepted Christ as my Savior. Soon afterwards my wife, too, was led to Christ. We had discovered that no one comes within arm's length of brother Pike without being touched by the Gospel! Since then, we have maintained an "inter-continental" friendship with this lovely family as they have commuted between South Africa, Australia and the United States. As an assistant editor on the mass-circulation *Sunday Times* newspaper, I have also been of some little assistance to the author in the preparation of three of his books, among them, *A History of Communism in South Africa*. Dr. Pike's dedication, over many years, to the fight against godless communism has always struck me as being unusually appropriate for someone who, in his own body and circumstances, has experienced such comprehensive suffering. The exquisite eulogy spoken by our risen Lord in Revelation 2:8-11 is climaxed by what is perhaps the most glorious assurance to the true believer to be found anywhere in Scripture. It applies as much to this dear brother as it did to the suffering Christians in Smyrna:

"Be thou faithful unto death, and I will give thee a crown of life."

DENIS HANDS, B.A.
Johannesburg
January 1, 1992

Chapter 1

Every Believer Has a Calling

Suffering, suffering, more suffering, then finally death! Would the average Christian be offended if I described these twins — suffering and death — as a vocation; even better, a divine calling direct from God? And that this calling should become the normal experience of every saved person who seeks to live a dedicated life of loving trust and obedience to the Savior?

The word "vocation" comes from the Latin word "vocare" meaning "to call." The Bible teaches that God sends holy callings to his children. Many are the divine subpoenas traveling from heaven to earth and into the hearts of the redeemed. There is a vast variety of callings. First, there is God's call to salvation or eternal life in Christ. This is described as "the heavenly calling" (Heb. 3:1); as being "called out of darkness into His (Christ's) marvelous light" (I Peter 2:9). It is a calling of "grace" (Gal. 1:15) and rests on the "faithfulness" of God Almighty (I Thess. 5:24). What greater security could be found?

After this summons to eternal life, given by the Holy Spirit and the Word of God, the saved Christian faces a variety of possible "vocares" from God. He calls some to preach, to teach, to sing, to construct buildings, to practice medicine, to rear children, to serve as foreign missionaries, and so forth. We have different callings or vocations in respect of our earthly jobs, professions and careers. The callings or "vocares" of which all believers are appointed to share are those of suffering and death. The only exceptions are those Christians living at the return of Christ. They will escape physical death, as their bodies will be instantly changed into bodies of glory and incorruption (I Cor. 15:51-54; Phil. 3:20-21 and Rom. 6:5).

1

God's holy calling to suffer and die is as much a part of His plan for our lives as a call to the ministry or mission field. It comes to every one of us and it comes from our kind, merciful and caring heavenly Father. But so very few of God's children understand it this way. The prevailing view of suffering and death among today's believers is distorted and even grossly misunderstood. We must recognize that they are ministries given to each of us, to be fulfilled for God in the highest honor and praise even, "To the only wise God our Savior . . ." (Jude 25).

We really learn nothing fresh and helpful about our Lord except through the deepest of sufferings and the darkest of sorrows; these gifts illuminate His Word and give life its unfeigned meaning.

When the Lord Jesus called the happy brothers James and John from their father's fishing enterprise, little did they know the future implications of their Master's call. We read of them these stirring words: "And they immediately left the ship and their father, and followed (Jesus)" (Matt. 4:22). Twelve years later, James finished his ministry when Herod's sword removed his head (Acts 12:1-2). Over sixty years later, John the elder was banished to the sufferings of Roman exile on the island called Patmos. This fifty-mile-square island was a prison where criminals were forced to work the mines for the Roman emperor. The very mention of Patmos caused brave men to shudder in horror.

From Galilee's peaceful shores to Herod's prison and the executioner's sword, the calling of James was completed and sealed with his life's blood. John outlived all the apostles and took his testimony of suffering for Christ to a bleak, rocky island where he gladly identified himself to his readers as their ". . . companion in tribulation" (Rev. 1:9). The "vocare" to which our Lord called the two brothers thus concluded. For the testimony of Christ one was executed and the other banished. God was glorified. Their highest calling was realized.

Regardless of the era in which we live, the origin of birth, our race, attitude of the State, our place of service, the theology we embrace, the love of neighbors and friends, how secure we may be financially, the peace of home, workplace and the mental contentment of good physical health, every child of God is still called along the road of suffering and death. However dark and terrible seems the fierce and howling seas that we must cross there is no danger, for God has willed it this way. Very often though, this is not so easily grasped. There may be times when God seems not to exist; even worse, when we know He exists but He seems not to care.

This latter truth is beautifully illustrated in Mark 4:35-41. The disciples had not put out to sea of their own decision; their Lord gave the order: ". . . Let us pass over unto the other side" (verse 35). The Savior was purposely leading them into a terrifying Galilean storm! On this water, travelers say, a vessel will be gliding along smoothly, over a glassy surface, when suddenly, without notice, a fierce tempest will assail the boat. Screaming, howling winds and mighty waves will threaten the destruction of all. We read of the disciples' little craft: "And there arose a great storm of wind, and the waves beat into the ship, so that it was now full" (verse 37). Jesus lay peacefully sleeping ". . . in the hinder part of the ship . . . on a pillow" (verse 38). It should be noted that the near presence of the Son of God does not keep the storm at bay. These terrified apostles were in that threatened boat only because Christ had commanded it. Hence, in the course of full obedience to our Lord's instructions, we too are frequently lashed by fierce storms. Trials bring us to our knees, crushing temptations seem to destroy every new resolution, sickness reduces us to ashes, and sorrows flood our souls. Often our life's allotment seems excessively harsh. And amid it all, God just can't be understood or figured out any longer. He won't make sense!

We must never conclude that we have taken the wrong path in Christian service when the storms fall suddenly upon us without warning. Oddly, that is the way God often works. Christ was there near His disciples only a few feet away! He was with them through it all. When a boat full of water (see Mark 4:37), will not sink, something wonderfully divine is about to happen.

3

Every child of God must travel with his Lord many times back and forth across the stormy Galilees of this world. Time-by-time, we glance down and stand horrified as we see our craft full of water. Surely it must sink! Our Savior appears uninterested. Still asleep on a pillow (verse 38). We wail the same foolish lament as the disciples of old, "Master, carest thou not that we perish?" (verse 38). Alas! when the cross demonstrates the depth of His care for our salvation and well being. Strangely, this is all part of our "vocare", part of our experience and calling from God.

Chapter 2

―――――――∙∙●€€€●●∙―――――――

Heresies Concerning Suffering And Death

Within the dark forbidden realm of the occult, demons have produced (I Tim. 4:1) curious and shocking doctrines concerning faith, sickness and healing. No longer, however, are weird and bizarre teachings confined to the kingdom of darkness. Now, the general public has been exposed for several decades to some of the broadest claims (all in the name of God or Christ) ever uttered regarding suffering, pain, sickness and death.

The "name-it-claim-it" cults and their offshoots, basically found within the wildest charismatic circles see suffering, pain, sickness and (often) death in a totally different light from otherwise, conservative Christians. The promising messages of these faith movements and churches appeals with magnetic passion to the fleshly emotions and theological ignorance of thousands of people. "God will always heal" and "God always wills to bless and prosper His children," so the attractive sermons go. One handbill attached to my car read: "God wants you to be rich and healthy. Come to the big tent. See the lame walk, the dumb talk, the deaf hear and the blind see." Such advertising carries a powerful attraction to the hard working, average man and woman, who have some vague knowledge that the Bible declares Christ performed such miracles while on earth. Countless thousands of sick and suffering persons, who have found no relief within the vast medical world, turn their hurting bodies and weary hearts to those who make these claims. "Everything else has failed surely God will help me," is the heart's cry of thousands.

In America, Australia, England, Canada, New Zealand, South Africa and other countries, some have gone so far as to teach that

5

if you die before the age of seventy years, you have died outside the will of God for your life! This alarming and impossible doctrine does not have its origin within the pages of Holy Scripture. Certain American charismatics, extremists of the worst sort, have carried this vicious lie around the world and there are always those who will embrace such rubbish with great zeal and enthusiasm. Other heretical complementary practices and teachings are lengthening short legs, filling decay holes in teeth, raising dead pets, knocking persons unconscious by blowing the breath, waving a hand or coat over them and so forth (II Cor. 11:14-15).

More pathetic than these shocking practices are the tragic thousands who dogmatically support such ballyhoo through attendance and finance. One is dismayed at the different manipulations, by means of which, such movements are born and thrive. Amid the tornado of pagan-style, often demonic jungle music, the adherents of such groups and churches are continually inflamed and swept into ecstatic pseudo-spiritual states. In this atmosphere, they usually exercise their "gifts of healing" and "claim prosperity and full health" for themselves and all "who can believe God for it." (As a foreign missionary, I have seen heathen witch-doctors perform similar musical rituals and make fantastic claims on behalf of demonic ancestral spirits.) Like the pagans, those who passively expose themselves to the psychological stimulant of mass chanting, singing, shouting and clapping — amid the frenzy of dancing, swaying, falling backwards, mingled with the brain-blasting beats of various percussion instruments are ready candidates for Satanic entrance and bondage of all sorts.

These cult adherents and their leaders fiercely cling to their unscriptural fraudulence even in the face of sickness, suffering and death affecting even their own loved ones. Worse, their failures are always explained away in terms of such quick-fit transparencies as: "They did not have faith" or "there was sin in their lives that prevented healing." Hitler's dictum — "inflame the masses and they will do anything" — works wonders even today in certain church circles. Hysteria, demonic or psychological, is the mother of many strange things, both possible and impossible!

The testimony of the Lord Jesus Christ and true Christianity in general, has suffered untold scorn and ridicule from such characters as Oral Roberts, (the late) Hobart Freeman, A.A. Allan and the kooky teachings of Kenneth Hagan, Robert Tilton and others of this ilk. Countless thousands of unsaved men, women and young people that should have been reached with the saving Gospel of Christ are now scandalized and totally alienated by the sheer hypocrisy of the Swaggart and Bakker affairs. The wicked have been given great occasion to blaspheme (II Sam. 12:14). Genuine Christianity is again trounced in the mud. The God hating world watches in glee as the modern day "spirit-filled", "tongues speaking" and "miracle working" Samsons go to bed with their motel room, strip-tease Delilahs. Then back to their T.V. preaching, churches and million dollar mansions — or prison. Thousands of unsaved sinners and dedicated saints both, have had enough of this sanctimonious charlatanry, deception, hypocrisy and masquerader type religion. Even the Godless unsaved world now sarcastically expresses its objections and contempt through the media.

Men who preach good and live bad should be banned from the pulpit by their churches, governing boards, overseers, and ecclesiastical hierarchy. They must never be allowed to return until there is genuine repentance of sin and corrective discipline applied in each case. This is the true process of Christian love as laid down in Scripture. It should be practiced across the board without respect to any person. But the wicked know it is not! One is prone to apply the old Hebrew proverb to these eccentrics who are forever "healing the sick" and performing "signs, wonders and miracles" and secretly (until they get caught) living like the Devil. It is recorded in Luke 4:23 and reads: "Physician, heal thyself . . ." (see Matt. 7:22-23). It must be stated that they all do not live such wicked double lives. But even those who do not, continually preach their absurd theology and inflame the innocent, seeking masses with their repugnant doctrines. Please, this is not mass condemnation of all charismatic believers.

7

God does not always "will" to heal the sick. Millions die before the age of seventy. The best of sinners and saints (even the prime-time T.V. faith healers) get sick, suffer pain, frustrations and confusion, lose their jobs, smash up their automobiles, become blind, deaf and dumb, die as a result of cancer, heart attacks, work accidents, polio, gunshot wounds, airplane crashes, blood poisoning, drowning, assaults, old age (even before seventy), and so forth. The claim that God in the Bible has promised to always give "health and wealth" to His obedient children is fraudulent and based on a foul exegesis of Holy Scripture. What is worse, these great claims do not even work in the lives of those who preach them. My personal physician (in South Africa), a Christian, shared with me how the local "famous faith-healing, prosperity pastor" secretly visited his office in need of medical attention for himself and one of his children! This was the same "man of God," who, after praying over a poor Down's syndrome child, told the shattered parent: "He is not healed because of your unbelief!" Today those embittered parents and that crushed mother hate the church. No wonder! Strange, that this super-healer's hot-line to heaven was foiled by the "unbelief" of another? (They quote Mark 6:5-6 to justify their failure.) And why was his child sick? That's easy. They cite John 9:3 for that one!

One cannot but ponder why the healing barons who advertise themselves as "ministering the power of Jesus" do not swoop into the nations' hospitals and perform their "signs, wonders and miracles"? Surely the love and compassion of Christ would mightily compel them into the institutions of terminal diseases, insane asylums, blind schools, the hundreds of Shriners and veterans hospitals scattered over the land, not to name the thousands of beds occupied by those dying with various fatal illnesses. However, they are not there producing their miracles and marvels. Neither will they ever be. Their absurd response to this mystery is not worth wasting space to print. Cold silence of performance in these critical areas alone and perpetual absenteeism proclaims these fabulous, mega-healers as phonies who cannot produce the goods to match the wonderful scriptures they quote.

8

The Son of God performed thousands of earth shaking miracles and wonders, healed all kinds of diseases and sicknesses, Himself said, that a sick man needs a physician (see Matt. 9:12). And surely the preachers and promoters of the extreme health-wealth abomination know that Jesus Christ died before He was seventy years old, not to mention scores of other great Christians over the course of church history. Suffering, sickness, trials and pain are part of the Christian life. Those who deny this are unrealistic and somehow dishonest with themselves and the human experience. Their super-spiritual claims may be sincere but they are also misleading, fallacious and treacherous.

There is little doubt that the most pitiful victims of the whole mess are the thousands of good, truly saved, well meaning and sincere Christians who are ensnared in these beliefs. Chained by pride, church loyalty, pseudo sincerity, the pressures of status quo, bonds of friendship and so on, thousands are locked into these strange doctrines. To dare question the validity of their pastors is cardinal sin (see John 9:22 and John 12:42). Should they fall seriously ill or suffer from financial pressures, they try to conceal such calamities from their spiritual peers for this would prove their lack of faith! Only when these people are willing to face life's realities and truth, then esteem the favor of God greater than the praise and compliments of men will they be delivered from these sects. To bear the criticism and scorn that goes with breaking from such errors is too much for most of them (see Rom. 16:17-18; II Cor. 6:14-18; 11:14-15; Gal. 1:6-8; Eph. 5:11-12; II Thess. 3:6-7; Titus 3:10-11; Heb. 13:9). These passages reveal what God has commanded about divisions and offenses against true doctrine, religious fellowship with unbelievers and efforts to mix spiritual light with spiritual darkness. They warn us that Satan comes as an angel of light, to reject all false gospels, do not fellowship with darkness, withdraw from those who walk disorderly, reject all heretics after the second warning and flee divers and strange doctrines. Only a badly informed or dishonest person would deny that the extreme, excessive and outrageous teachings of the groups mentioned surely fall within the embrace of these passages from

Holy Scripture.

In reality the weird and impossible teachings of these mixed up people slams straight into the face of the Bible truth, that God has called His children into lives that lead them into unspeakable sufferings and sorrows. At times their lot will fall upon deep heartache, frustration, pain and even certain physical sickness — or death. For this is their "vocare" (their calling) sent from above. At least one of Job's miserable comforters spoke the truth when he said: "Yet man is born unto trouble, as the sparks fly upward" (Job 5:7). Later on in this drama we hear Job lament: "Man that is born of a woman is of few days, and full of trouble" (Job 14:1). Over the course of true religious history, God's response to the sufferings and problems of His people has never changed: "I will be with him in trouble . . ." (Psa. 91:15). There is a wonderful bright side to our "vocare"! It is true because God said so.

Chapter 3

Faith Now Sits on the Throne Of God

As surely as our Lord has appointed His children to vocations that inevitably include suffering, pain, sickness and death, so surely has the Devil invented and is propagating an appealing alternative to the purposes and counsel of the Almighty. A popular British preacher once said: "While truth puts her shoes on, lie goes round the world." Consequently, mass error concerning suffering, sickness and death is abundant. The prime danger lies in the fact that all of these cunning doctrinal corruptions are so thoroughly integrated with fragments of popular and basic Bible doctrines that it takes an experienced Christian, one highly skilled in God's Word, to detect the difference. It is on this very point that the cults make such easy prey of the sincerely interested (but scripturally ignorant) masses. The truths they do preach and teach, so often have hidden hooks couched within the appealing bait. And history affirms the anxious masses swallow the bait.

Without fail, such movements accentuate the subject of "faith." Frequently, we hear their "ministers" preaching this Bible subject in the highest grandeur of human language. Then I am reminded that one of the ancients said: "Elegance from the mouth of a wicked man is like poison from a golden cup." Continually they claim: "If you have faith you can remove mountains" (these mountains are usually financial ruin, serious illness, domestic problems and so forth). The obvious implication is that faith (if you can get it) guarantees smooth sailing through whatever problems. Another favorite term is: "You need the faith that can get whatever it asks for" (based on Mark 9:23). And of course Hebrews 11:6 is the overshadowing passage in all their mythology; it reads: "But without faith it is impossible to please God . . . ." Their usage of

11

these and numerous other verses produces in the minds of the audience a sense of guilt; a feeling of deep inferiority. The psychological overtone is: "I am a weak Christian. If I had this kind of faith I would never have these problems in life." Hearing these glorious claims from Holy Scripture the average Christian thinks this is the whole story; this is all he needs to make life full and successful. Then he sets out on the great adventure to acquire this superior faith in God. A few years later the aftermath is appalling in the lives of hundreds of these sincere people, as they begin to discover life still has its pains, sicknesses, trials, financial strains and unsolved problems. Then falls "the straw that broke the camel's back." These poor souls are reminded by their spiritual leaders that "it has not worked, because you did not have faith or there is sin in your life!" The standard cop-out.

But there is another side to this sinful saga. Only a fool would explain away the Bible teachings regarding faith. And just as extreme are those who preach the "faith in faith" philosophy. Scripturally, our experience from the moment of salvation till we reach heaven and home, is continuously based on faith. We are saved by faith (Eph. 2:8-9). Then we are to walk by faith (II Cor. 5:7). We live by faith (Gal. 3:11). Faith for daily living comes from God's Word (Matt. 4:4 with Rom. 10:17). Satan must be resisted by faith and the correct use of the Word of God (I Peter 5:8-9 with Eph. 6:16 and James 4:7). Faith exercised in harmony with God's will covers us like the Roman military shield (Eph. 6:6). Lost souls are only saved through repentance and faith in the finished work of Christ (Lk. 13:3; Acts 13:38-39; 17:30-31; 20:21 with Rom. 10:9). Only by this kind of faith do men become the children of God (Gal. 3:26). All prayer must be "in the Spirit" (Eph. 6:18), directed by simple faith that God's final will be done (I John 5:14-15). The greatest of faith will not move God to give what He has not willed for His child to have (II Cor. 12:7-10). Faith is not "hitting the jackpot," that's gambling! Paul said it is seeing the unseen (Heb. 11:1) and receiving it, when God wills it so (see Eph. 5:17; Acts 21:14; Heb. 6:3 and I John 5:14-15).

Amid the heated atmosphere of wild extremism (especially in

religion and politics) almost anything is possible. Over the past decade or so, there has risen within this climate one of the most audacious and impudent teachings ever heard. It is a subversion of the doctrine of faith; even an attempted demonic coup staged upon this truth of God's Word. Now "lord Faith" is being placed on the throne of God. The American charismatic pastor, Fred Price, is a classic, but not isolated example of this corruption of established Bible doctrine. Preaching to thousands at Oral Roberts University in Tulsa, Oklahoma, Price rocked his audience with this blasphemy: "It is not God that heals, but faith." (Instantly he was challenged from the floor by a professor who knew better!) To show the reader just how far this absurd type of preaching-teaching has gone, Oral Roberts himself, seated on the stage, leapt to his feet and demanded an apology from the angry professor. At the conclusion of the message, Price received a "standing ovation" as an expression of appreciation for his preaching.

Price and Roberts are not alone in their clap-trap exegesis of Holy Scripture. They have plenty of company especially within the realms of the radical, healing-prosperity sects, all of them operating under the umbrella of "Bible Christianity." Only sick theology could conjure up such claims for Bible faith. Does faith really have power to heal the sick? Price even quotes a verse to "prove" his folly; Christ's words to the woman just healed: "Thy faith hath made thee whole" (Lk. 8:48). What happened to God's sovereignty over all things? Even a thoughtful Sunday School child knows better than Price. It was through this woman's faith in God that her body was healed. Not her faith in faith.

True faith has as its noble objects, God and His divine will. Faith is the channel to the Person — God. Jesus said: "Have faith in God" (Mark 11:22). Faith's target is the loving heart of God. Its motive is for His will to be done. In the garden of agony Christ prayed: ". . . not my will but thine be done" (Lk 22:42). If one had faith to literally move mountains (and God was pleased to do so) that would never change the fact that Christians are called into lives of suffering, heartache, trials and finally death. Missionary Paul was surely a man of faith. Read the list of mountains that it did not

13

move from his life (II Cor. 11:21-33).

Contrary wise, the sufferings of this life, our trials and storms serve to give faith its true meaning. The only faith that will finally satisfy the soul's need is that which has passed through deep sorrows, self agony, the unanswered heartaches of human life and has survived them all.

Faith is not a blank check filled in for whatever we want from God. It is not a shotgun that we brandish in God's face and demand of Him our human fancies. Faith is not the "lucky number" nor is faith "striking it rich." Bible faith is a clinging trust that madly believes in our loving heavenly Father, both when we understand and things are well, and when we cannot understand and nothing seems well. Often our faith is so fiercely tried that it appears like the barren fig tree of Luke 13:6-9. Fruitless, unable to produce, waiting for the keeper's axe to cut it down; such faith can only drop dying leaves to the ground in hope that God makes these a carpet on which the elect may walk and find comfort for tired feet. Faith tries to see something that will be done when everything about screams nothing can be done. This is not the cheap vulgarized version of faith preached by the cults who gloat in their "success and fame" and point to their big numbers and material gain as "proof of God's blessings," while perverting Holy Scripture amid the whole sickening process.

But there will be times in the lives of the best of Christians when even trusting God seems impossible. All who follow their Lord will at some stage experience what the woman experienced who continually begged Christ to heal her daughter: "But He answered her not a word" (Matt. 15:23). These deathly quiet seasons, when God becomes still and silent are almost unbearable, yet are part of our divine vocation. Great is the need to remind our faint hearts that ". . . in quietness and confidence shall be your strength" (Isa. 30:15). However, it is not always so easy to do. The quietness of God can be so easily misinterpreted. Martin Luther prayed out of his frustrations: "O God judge us but please don't be silent." We bear pain better than silence.

14

To preach that it is not God that heals but our faith is to preach appalling untruth. It is to transfer God's right and choice into the hands of a non-person. Faith in faith is a doctrine alien to Holy Scripture. It is the by-product of radical extremism, the fruit of the depraved flesh and possibly springs from demonic reasoning. We refuse to be so ignorant as to substitute our faith for the work that only God can do. The faith we do have is wrought in our hearts by hearing God's Word (Rom. 10:17). Even our desperate, clinging, importunate prayers of faith, can only move God to grant what He wills that such praying can have (see examples of this in Luke 11:1-10 and Luke 18:1-8). According to Isaiah 6:1, it was the "Lord sitting upon a throne," and not charismatic faith. Some 700 years later, it was still the Lord sitting upon the dazzling, rainbow-encircled throne of Revelation 4:2-3. He has not vacated His sovereign position. He alone decrees what shall be.

Let Price and Roberts make their lunatic claims about the source of true healing. While they rattle off, God said to Israel in the wilderness: "I am the Lord that healeth thee" (Ex. 15:26). Faith has never been enthroned nor does it heal. Only the Eternal One has this sovereignty. How thankful God's informed people are for this consoling realization. Our faith may oft collapse (see Lk 22:32), but never our heavenly Father. Alas! can we fail to remember (and we do) that God is never so near, as when He seems so painfully absent. Meek, child-like faith is the bridge that transports us to the loving heart of our loving Lord. Amid whatever experiences in our lives God's choice may bring upon us; blessing or burden, darkness or light, comfort or silence, healing or hardship, joy or sorrow, gain or loss, life or death; whatever the divine choice is — God always does right.

Even in the overwhelming severity of life's most crushing struggles, when our child-like faith cannot be found, God's word still offers this sure hope: "If we believe not, yet He abideth faithful . . ." (II Tim. 2:13). When shuddering sorrows cloud the bridge that directs us to our Lord — He is still faithful!

Informed Christians reject and contend against the faith in faith philosophy being preached as sound Bible doctrine. Our

15

calling or "vocare" from God directs us into life and this is filled with sorrows, sufferings, troubles, heartaches, pain and sickness and finally physical death. The promises of the big noise Faith movements about life's "smooth sailing" are nothing short of cunning untruths couched in foul-exegeted passages excerpted from Holy Scripture. Faith does not sit on the throne of God, has never performed a single miracle, sign or wonder. Nor will it ever.

Chapter 4

Men of Faith Who Temporarily Lost Faith

Dare any of us be so brave as "the weeping prophet" and blurt out our frustrations and innermost hatred to God as he did? Read the shocking confession of Jeremiah: "Mine heritage is unto me as a lion in the forest; it crieth out against me: therefore have I hated it. Mine heritage is unto me as a speckled bird, the birds around about are against her . . ." (Jer. 12:8-9). I can honestly state that I have felt exactly the same way! Our "heritage" is our salvation, our hope and our work, our calling from God. The "vocare" of each child of God is found within our heritage. Fellow Christian, if you sincerely desire to know the Lord and attempt to do His will for your life, you too, will strangely find times when the lament of Jeremiah will be your own. These certain and awesome experiences of the Christian life are denied by those who "always live in a super faith" and tell us that "with true belief in Christ," one cannot possibly be subject to such times and experiences.

Such death-like ordeals are part of our heavenly assignment. We must bear them with holy dignity and esteem. Others cannot share this load. Is it not written: "For every man shall bear his own burden" (Gal. 6:5)? Then, there are other heartaches and trials that fellow Christians may help us carry: "Bear ye one another's burdens, and so fulfil the law of Christ" (Gal. 6:2). Our Lord Himself will take many of them: "Cast thy burden upon the Lord . . ." (Psa. 55:22 with I Peter 5:7). But there are others that we must bear alone. Only by a determined perseverance can we bear such burdens. God has planned it this way. It is within this realm that our heritage is like the pitiful "speckled bird," being picked to bleeding and often death by the birds round about that are against her. Jeremiah, so crushed under his sorrows, replied: "Therefore have I hated it." One wonders where the great prophet's faith was? Probably the same place as ours when we suffer similar trials.

We would disdain to honor unbelief and the sinful lack of faith or a wicked distrust in God's Word. At the same time, however, we must face honestly the realities in the lives of everyday, normal Christians. The "speckled bird" encounters will be numerous; so numerous that some will hate them. The forest of life is filled with lions. O how they roar against us! This is but part of the calling of God's children. History tells that all share in it. Moses has been recognized as the greatest single leader in human experience. Yet, he found himself so downcast, so distressed, so frustrated and weary of life's load that he prayed God to kill him: "I am not able to bear all this people alone, because it is too heavy for me. And if thou deal thus with me, kill me, I pray thee, out of hand . . ." (Num. 11:14-15). Moses did not always exercise supernatural, abounding faith in Jehovah God (amazingly, see with this Heb. 11:24-29). Did you ever feel like Moses?

Elijah has been described as the "Greatest prophet in the Old Testament." His faith, exercised in believing prayer, is spoken of by James: ". . . (Elijah) prayed earnestly that it might not rain: and it rained not on the earth by the space of three years and six months. And he prayed again, and the heaven gave rain, and the earth brought forth her fruit" (James 5:17-18). But even the powerful Elijah fell — crushed by despair and fears. After the astounding victory over the Devil's prophets on Mt. Carmel, mighty Elijah fled in terror from the threats of a godless woman named Jezebel. Exhausted and flat on his back under the shade of a juniper tree, he calls on God to kill him: "It is enough; now, O Lord, take my life . . ." (I Kings 19:4). How many times in my own weariness I have said: "It is enough." The man who had faith one day to pray down a three-and-a-half-year drought, had no faith the next. Sound familiar?

It is probably when our sorrows and sufferings seem to have no reason or meaning that we sink into the pit of overwhelming despair. Job is introduced as no other man in the Holy Bible: ". . . and that man was perfect and upright, and one that feared God, and eschewed (shunned) evil" (Job 1:1). According to both God and Satan, there was no man on earth like Job in his era (Job 2:3-4). Yet, when his life seemed to collapse, everything he loved vanished, sorrows and grief covered him as a flood, even Job cursed the day on which he was born. (Job 3:1-26). His faith in the Almighty sank to its lowest level. This ". . . greatest of all the men of the east" (Job 1:3), hit the solid bottom! Many Christians have experienced something of the same. Every child of God who has walked with his Lord, feels a curious affinity with Job as he struggled with his calamities and unanswered prayer (Job 6:8). Did not Jeremiah likewise curse the day of his birth (Jer. 20:14-15,18), when his sorrows became unbearable? This too, sounds familiar.

Conservative Bible scholars estimate that John the Baptist preached about one year and six months before being imprisoned by Herod. A survey of John's preaching and description of the Lord Jesus is marvelous. In (seemingly) unshakable confidence John proclaimed Christ as the greatest (John 3:31), "the final judge" (Matt. 3:12), "the one who baptises with the Holy Spirit" (Lk 3:16), "light for men" (John 1:7), "the true light" (John 1:9), "the Lamb of God, which taketh away the sin of the world" (John 1:29), the one to whom the Father had "given all things" (John 3:35) and the one in whom men must believe to be saved from God's wrath (John 3:36). Few preachers have, in such short time, ever exalted Christ like John the Baptist. Time changes things. John was arrested and thrown into the fearful and greatly dreaded Dead Sea prison. Here he languished for at least a year. Many students of the Bible are shocked to read John's words after this year of indescribable suffering in Herod's torture house waiting for the executioner's sword to lift his head. "Now when John had heard in prison the works of Christ, he sent two of his disciples, And said unto (Jesus), Art thou he that should come, or do we look for another?" (Matt. 11:2-3). One is prone to ask where was his great faith in Jesus? Why this sudden change of opinion? What had happened to this mighty man of God? Had he preached one thing and now practiced another?

Suffering, prison, mental torments and more had done

something seriously strange to this great preacher and forerunner of the Messiah. Apparently, he simply doubted some of his former statements and declarations about the Lord Jesus. He was devastated by his sufferings. Now a broken spirit speaks, not a powerful evangelist. There is a shocking difference! Over the course of Church history millions of Christians have passed over John's road. Have you drunk from his cup? His was not an announcement of apostasy, bitter rejection, or even sinful, wicked, deliberate unbelief. It is the sob of a thoroughly broken preacher; at wits end, reaching out for help, answers and fresh hope. Most of the faithful ministers, missionaries, Bible teachers and pastors with whom I am acquainted, have all shared in John's utter despair. I surely have. He was fulfilling his divine "vocare," the way of God for his life. No sold out Christian escapes passing this way. Those who do have a cheap vulgarity over their ministries. They are shallow and empty, though often flashy and full of words, yet miserably void of God's power.

What was the response of Christ to John's (sinless) dilemma and frustration? Our blessed Savior responded in love and sympathetic understanding. He even praised John as "more than a prophet" (Matt. 11:9), even as the greatest man born of woman (Matt. 11:11). Jesus did not chide with him but spoke words of comfort to the bewildered preacher. Christ understood. Likewise, He tenderly understands our frustrations and fears.

The greatest men of Holy Scripture experienced times in their work and ministries when faith seemed to fail. Every Christian will eventually suffer similar days and nights in their own lives. Scripture bristles with this lesson. Woe betide those who fail to grasp it.

The dark experiences of Moses, Elijah, Job, Jeremiah and John are similarly ours also — the only difference being — our's are written in a longer text. Men of faith also have temporarily lost their faith. What a cheerful encouragement to us who are not classified as "the greatest men of Holy Scripture." Perhaps we are not doing so bad after all!

Suffering is universal to every true child of God. If you are a servant of the living Christ, you too must be tried — as gold is tried. It is part of your divine calling. And in a majestic sense — almost sacred — somehow, God's glory shines through His suffering, weeping saints.

The billion tears of Christians, shed over the span of earth's sorrowing night, now hang as shadowed dew drops on every flower, stone, blade and tree. But yonder in that dawning eternal era to come, they shall sparkle like diamonds in heaven's endless day.

Chapter 5

Paul's Faith and the Saints of Hebrews 11

The Christian's life of faith is not always constant or consistent, despite the bold statements of some who preach on national T.V. and in packed stadiums. Our faith often wavers. It rises and falls between experiences of supreme exaltation and utter despair. Paul's faith in God and His will produced staggering miracles during the "high experiences" of his missionary work (Acts 13:11-12; 14:3, 6-10; 19:12; Rom. 15:18-19). Then Paul found himself (upon entering Asia) so pressed out of measure that he ". . . despaired even of life" (II Cor. 1:8-10). How many of my readers have "despaired even of life"? At no time did God rebuke Paul for such "mood swings" in his missionary experiences. He was only being normal. Beware of those "spiritual leaders" who condemn God's people for being normal Christians.

Rare, if not non-existent, is the Christian who has a tranquil spirit and mind at all times and in all seasons. No clearer picture of this fact is found anywhere in the New Testament than in Paul's confession of his own feelings and fears. In the passage quoted above (II Cor. 1:8), the apostle candidly says of himself that when he went into Asia (on his second missionary journey) He ". . . despaired even of life." Bear in mind, this is the man that had seen the Lord Jesus and was given unique visions and revelations of the things of God (I Cor. 9:1; II Cor. 12:1-4; Gal. 1:11-12; Eph. 3:1-4). Lo, now he flounders in the pit of despair! A few pages further on in the same letter, Paul refers to his life in general as a preacher of the Gospel and declared that he is ". . . troubled on every side, yet not distressed . . . (and) perplexed but not in despair" (II Cor. 4:8). In chapter one he is wallowing in despair; in chapter four, he rises above it! There is no contradiction here; rather a crystal-clear explanation of the fact that the greatest men of God have their times of crushing despair, and their times of exultant victory. We all go this way. It is part of our calling from God. Our "vocare" surely includes these "ups and downs." They are not a genuine reflection of our spiritual temperature or fellowship with God. They are natural. Flee from those who preach against being natural.

One wonders (according to the doctrine of the "name-it-claim-it" cults) where Paul's faith was when he suffered the "many perils, weariness, painfulness, hunger, cold, thirst and nakedness" listed in II Corinthians 11:26-27. When we recall that this is the same Paul who wrote: "But my God shall supply all your need according to His riches in glory by Christ Jesus" (Phil. 4:19), we are simply staggered. One cannot help but wonder what he was doing "cold, hungry and naked." Perhaps he needed to study the writings of Hobart Freeman, William Brannan or Kenneth Hagan. Regarding his horrible "thorn in the flesh" (II Cor. 12:1-10), surely if he had only studied Oral Roberts' best seller, "If You Need Healing, Do These Things," his problem would have been solved instantly. Speaking in a courteous but satirical manner, one is prone to think, that it would seem to be nothing short of disaster for the cause of Christ that the greatest missionary in human history did not know the "doctrine of claiming your health by faith," or that Paul did not utter the spoken word of authority ("rhema") and consequently live in the prosperity that such miracles supposedly provide. If only the apostle had practiced such a "life of faith" he would surely never have experienced the physical sufferings and sorrows that he listed as part of his ministry (see II Cor. 4:8-12; 6:4-10; 11:23-33 and 12:1-10 for the full catalogue). The contrary is however, true: every saved Christian who follows hard after his Lord (Psa. 63:8) for any reasonable period, learns that the highway to heaven is paved with blood, sweat and tears. Why? Because of God's calling upon His own — the "vocare" of our shared ministry, the divine summons to suffering, sorrow and finally physical death. Even our Lord was described as ". . . a man of sorrows and acquainted with grief" (Isa. 53:3). Can we be less? His obedience carried Him to the greatest of all sufferings, ". . . even the death of the cross" (Phil. 2:8). The cults tell us that obedience and faith will carry one into the heights of plenty, prosperity and material power; all so alien to Bible Christianity.

Truly the ex-fisherman spoke profoundly when he said: "For even hereunto were ye called: because Christ also suffered for us, leaving us an example, that ye should follow His steps" (I Peter 2:21). No believer who follows "His steps" can avoid suffering, sorrow, sickness, pain and finally death. It is the ordained lot of our common humanity and faith, even part of our heavenly calling. Those who deny this obvious reality of life and faith, this glaring fact established in two thousand years of Christian history, are woefully ignorant and somehow ". . . are the enemies of the cross of Christ" (Phil. 3:18). Their sincerity is not questioned, but their presentation of truth in these areas, their insight into the human experience and their understanding of the Holy Scriptures certainly are questionable.

The long list of faith's heroes and heroines, recorded in Hebrews 11, would stand up poorly within many of today's "Christian Centers," "Healing Tabernacles," "Rock Churches," "Rhema Assemblies" with their various mixtures of apostasy, liberalism, ecumenicalism and the ultra radical healing, prosperity doctrines. Their lives and experiences were so contrary to what is frequently presented as "faith" and "truth" by these groups. Yet, the Bible clearly presents these as exemplary examples of faith. Each individual in Hebrews 11 lived a life of suffering and sorrow, mingled with victory and triumph. Not one "prosperity saint" (in terms of the absurd standards of today's groups) can be found among that triumphant army of saints in Hebrews 11.

Again, the contrary is true: none of these champions of the faith are characterized by their wealth and prosperity, but rather, by what they suffered and endured because of their faith. We read: ". . . others were tortured, not accepting deliverance . . . others had trial of cruel mockings and scourgings, yea, moreover of bonds and imprisonment; They were stoned, they were sawn asunder, were tempted, were slain with the sword: they wandered in deserts, and in mountains, and in dens and caves of the earth." Despite their prayers God saw fit not to deliver them from terrible sufferings (see Heb. 11:35-37). This is a vastly different scene from that painted by the "wealthy-healthy-prosperity" sects of modern day Christianity. The eight-bedroom, five-bathroom, four-garage, twenty-acre mansions; the $1,000.00 suits, the $5,000.00 Rolex watches and executive automobiles (so we are told), prove "God's blessings on their lives and ministries." One Johannesburg "Spirit filled" pastor, prancing across the platform, slobbering on the handmike, lifting and swinging his feet and knees in military-drill fashion, declared that his material acquisitions amounted to God honoring his faith with a ". . . good measure, pressed down, shaken together, and running over . . ." (Luke 6:38). At the conclusion of this glorious declaration the whipped-up, frenzied crowd was instructed to "Give Jesus a hand," which they did with a thunderous roar of applause. (Note the public Hebrew custom of clapping hands in Psalm 47:1, contrasted with Paul's lucid words regarding NOT worshipping God ". . . with men's hands" in Acts 17:24-25.)

If "things" and "material goods" exhibit God's blessings and approval on one's life then the Mafia in Sicily, the Rockefellers in New York, the cut-throat money lords and drug barons of South America, the Kennedys in Massachusetts, and even the heartless rich man of Luke 16:19-31 are all blessed and approved of God. Such reasoning is ridiculous, if not deranged. (Concerning the prosperity of the wicked, see Psalm 49:16-20 and James 5:1-4).

It must be noted that the saints of Hebrews 11 have a glorious heavenly benediction pronounced over their lives: "Of whom the world was not worthy" (verse 38). Quite a different story from today's so-called "anointed," "blessed" and "mightily used Christian leaders," who glory in their luxury and fame, court the friendship and support of godless apostates and shift their failures in praying for the sick and suffering onto (the already hurting) innocent bystanders.

Success in the Christian life, the pastorate, in Bible college, on the daily job, the foreign mission field, or where ever, is measured by God in a vastly different way than the super-saints of the wealthy-healthy syndrome measure such things. Success in following the Lamb of God will not transform you into a millionaire Christian, a religious Hollywood playboy, the most popular preacher or evangelist of the year. Nay, rather it will sweep you into a life of self-death, suffering and trials. Even a daily nailing to the old rugged cross, sharing in its agony and pain, feeling the weight of its load and the shame of its stigma. To suffer with Christ is nobler than to reign as king. Its riches and wealth endure for ever. Every time in our Christian experience we are called upon to "go down into Egypt," we should carry the hope that in God's time, we will march out ladened with gold, silver and precious stones. These spoils not of material endurance, mystically and wonderfully are conforming us to the image of Christ our Lord (Rom. 8:28-29).

Chapter 6

————◦•◦◦✦◦◦•◦————

True Prosperity And Some Men Who Fell Ill

Blessings and prosperity as mentioned in Holy Scripture should not be measured in terms of pastors' palaces, great crowds, curvaceous glamour-girl wives and luxurious mansions on the beach. God's true blessings and approval are not unalterably expressed in stocks and bonds, high interest rates gained, flamboyant sports cars, jet-setting across the globe "to lecture," and heaven-signed guarantees of no sickness, suffering, loss and doubts, or (as the Australians say) "pie in the sky."

Various men in the Bible to whom God entrusted great riches (such as Abraham, David, Solomon, Joseph of Arimathaea) not once boasted of their wealth as proof of God's favor. Scriptures teach that some rich men may indeed have faith, but there is always the hovering danger of trusting in their wealth instead of the Living God (see I Tim. 6:17 with Matt. 19:23-24). The sense of security that money and its power offers must be handled with the most extreme caution, kept under strict discipline and always subjugated to a simple trust for life and being from the Almighty. I have met men of wealth who were fools enough to believe the insanity that King Solomon temporarily fell victim to: ". . . but money answereth all things" (Eccl. 10:19). One wonders what money will answer to God's judgment bar?

According to the contexts of both Psalms 37 and 73, the godless prosper, increase their riches and power, but are not in trouble like other men; yet, they know not the Lord and live in fat (Psa. 17:8-10) unbelief. Could such prosperity be proof of God's blessings? Impossible! James the half-brother of our Savior, wrote: "Hearken, my beloved brethren, Hath not God chosen the poor of this world rich in faith, and heirs of the kingdom which He hath promised to them that love Him" (James 2:5). As just mentioned, King Solomon after learning the hard way could write: "How much better is it to get wisdom than gold" (Prov. 16:16). Just before they entered the promised land of Canaan, God sternly warned Israel concerning the snare of the prosperity that waited for them (see Deut. 8:10-18). Possibly the best balance between prosperity and poverty is recorded in Ecclesiastes 7:14: "In the day of prosperity be joyful, but in the day of adversity (poverty and leanness) consider: God also hath set one over the other . . . ." Surely, the writer is saying that in times of plenty we should exercise great self-control, and in adversity one's behavior should be that of deep thoughtfulness and reflection. Neither state is considered sinful; but correct behavior is advised for both situations in life.

The beautiful text of II Corinthians 8:9 is so often abused by the prosperity cults: "For ye know the grace of our Lord Jesus Christ, that, though he was rich, yet for your sakes he became poor, that ye through his poverty might be rich." This hardly has reference to Wall Street in New York, or your local Stock Market. Those who preach financial wealth through this verse, do great dishonor to sacred Scripture and bring serious reproach upon true Christianity and its purpose in the world. (Concerning riches of everlasting quality see Rom. 2:4; Eph. 1:7,18; 2:4; 3:8; Phil. 4:19; Heb. 11:26 and I Peter 1:3-4.)

But there is another side to the story. I have also met a few lovely Christians who were wealthy and increased in this world's goods. They have money, but money does not have them. It is their servant not their master. They are described in Proverbs 15:6, "In the house of the righteous is much treasure . . ." (in the context this passage is speaking of financial accruement). A distinguishing feature of saved, dedicated and informed Christians who have great wealth, is, they never point to their riches and power as evidence that their faith is superior or that they are superlative believers of Batman variety. A rich Australian sheep farmer once told me he frequently cited to himself the sobering passage: "Naked came I out of my mother's womb, and naked shall I return thither . . ." (Job

1:21). This meek Christian gentleman pungently remarked: "I have noticed when a man dies his hands open!"

Earthly riches no more prove an abundance of faith than poverty proves a lack of faith. King Solomon, the richest man in all human history, had enough sense to write: "The rich and the poor meet together: the Lord is the maker of them all" (Prov. 22:2). (Those who have been seriously enchanted by the "wonderful promises" of the healing-prosperity teachers would do well to locate a Strong's Exhaustive Concordance and check each of the thirty-seven references to the word "poor" found in the book of Proverbs alone.) All men — rich, poor and in between — would do well to remember God's solemn claim in Haggai 2:8: "The silver is mine, and the gold is mine, saith the Lord of hosts." It is beyond doubt that some men have acquired their wealth through a horrible alliance with the Devil (see Matt. 4:8-9). In the life which is to come they will also receive full interest from the hand of God (Matt. 25:41-46; James 5:1-3; Rev. 6:15-17).

The hallmark of a genuine Christian consists not in the figures in his bank book, his social status, the price of his automobile, the expensive dresses his wife wears or the exquisite furnishings of an exotic palace, but in the depth and sincerity of his love for God. It is from this basic foundation that real Christianity lives, thrives, works and succeeds. Our Savior declared: "By this (not wealth) shall all men know that ye are my disciples, if ye have love one to another" (John 13:35). Divine love is the acid-test of true Christianity. Paul wrote: ". . . if any man love God, the same is known of him" (I Cor. 8:3). To pursue God madly with a burning passion and reckless abandon love has been the compelling dynamic of true Christianity over the centuries. Love is our banner and I.D.

In view of the preposterous claims made by the "never sick" and "never broke" adherents one wonders how that mighty prophet Elisha would have fared as a member of their organizations. He died sick (see II Kings 13:14). The poor fellow! If only he "had faith," he would surely not have died of his sickness, or so we are hearing. Too bad someone did not mail him "a prayer cloth"

31

anointed by one of today's "miracle" healers or a recording of Oral Robert's deliverance testimony. To "die sick" is clearly a crime, by their standards. Yet some eight-hundred years after Elisha's death, the Son of God spoke of him in high regard "Eliseus the prophet" (Lk 4:27). Is it possible that some saints die sick? Elisha did! And God promised Israel He would smite them with sickness (Mic. 6:13).

For Paul to have left ". . . Trophimus . . . at Miletum sick" (II Tim. 4:20) is a mystery indeed, since (we are told) "God wills all to be healed." Of course, the prosperity-healing cults, never short of facile explanations, have a ready-made response, "God was willing to heal him, but Trophimus did not have the faith"! (They are brazen enough to preach that Job suffered what he did because of his "fears" and "unbelief." And they quote Job 3:25 to prove their clap trap.)

Others in Scripture who were sick, but of whose healing no mention is made, were Jacob (Gen. 48:1), the "poor man" (Psa. 41:1,3), Daniel (Dan. 8:27) and Paul's missionary companion, Epaphroditus, who was critically ill through overwork (Phil. 2:25-30). Most conspicuous, Paul himself suffered from a mysterious physical infirmity that kept him weak and humble (II Cor. 10:10; Gal. 4:12-15; II Cor. 11:17 and 12:7-10). If sickness is a sin and always proof of disobedience then how could the Lord Jesus Christ say (even in figurative language) that He was "sick" in Matthew 25:34-40? Is Christ saying that He had sinned? Or that He had been disobedient to the Father? Such reasoning borders on blasphemy.

Bible scholars of the highest academic and spiritual calibre have continually noted that the healing cult leaders spontaneously quote and apply numerous passages from Scripture without consideration of the established rules of sound exegesis or hermeneutics. They neglect historical, social, contextual and grammatical realities. The primary passages these people use to prove their claims are Ex. 15:26; Deut. 7:15; Psa. 103:3; Matt. 4:23; 8:17; 21:22; Mk. 9:23; John 14:12-14; Acts 10:38; I Cor. 12:9; Heb. 13:8; Jam. 5:14-15 and III John 2. Contrary to the radical claims of these groups, King Solomon described one of life's most observable facts: "All things come alike to all: there is one event to the righteous, and to the wicked; to the good and to the clean, and to the unclean; to him that sacrificeth, and to him that sacrificeth not: as is the good, so is the sinner; and he that sweareth, as he that sweareth not" (Eccl. 9:2). Sickness like perspiration is one of the common lots of our shared humanity. It is part of our calling as we pass through this life, dwelling in physical houses of clay cursed by sin.

Scripture commands that God's children should be disenfranchised from this world. Though living in it, appreciating its good (I John 3:17), seeking to obey its laws (Rom. 13:1-8 and Titus 3:1), respecting our superiors (I Peter 2:17) and trying to live peaceably with all men (Rom. 12:18), our salvation and calling declares that we should be a peculiar people (Titus 2:14). Our final destination distinctively sets us apart from the unsaved (II Peter 3:13). In view of the eternity that awaits the born-again Christian, he can gladly be identified as a stranger and pilgrim on earth (Heb. 11:13), looking for a city whose builder and maker is God (Heb. 11:10). We serve the King men did not enthrone and therefore cannot dethrone. Pilate, in a frantic effort to free himself from the wrath of Caesar and the Roman Senate, scribbled on the cross: "THIS IS THE KING OF THE JEWS" (Lk. 23:38). Indeed, a poor if not sickly designation for true deity. But heaven will correct what man corrupts. Over sixty years later, in apocalyptic glory and terror, Almighty God correctly designates His Son's absolute regal and political status: "And He hath on His vesture and on His thigh a name written, KING OF KINGS, AND LORD OF LORDS" (Rev. 19:16). Now the story is clear. Now the truth is known. He is not just THE KING OF THE JEWS. He is THE KING and THE LORD over all kings and lords of all time.

Because THE KING has saved us and called us, we must understand that our passing through earth's little day of necessity carries with it a mirrored reflection of His likeness. As He was in the world, so are we. This likeness is especially shown in our sufferings, sorrows, trials, and griefs. But with a unique, grand and different significance. They are divinely given to all saints, some with more, others with less, but all with sovereign design and purpose. A good thing will eventually come out of our every Nazareth (John 1:46). Each of life's bitter Marahs, will, in time, be turned into sweetness by the tree of the cross (Ex. 15:23-25). Only a fool would "look back" on the cesspool of a burning Sodom and long for its shameful lusts (Gen. 19:24-25 with Luke 17:32). All the majesty of this noisy alluring world is nothing but an empty pageant, meaningless and vain. The saint's "vocare" leads to suffering and this suffering should produce the summa cum laude upon their life's thesis. For this thesis is being written with the ink of tears, sufferings, joy and love.

Chapter 7

A Football Accident: God Tackled me

"Before I was afflicted I went astray: but now have I kept thy word" (Psa. 119:67). "It is good for me that I have been afflicted: that I might learn thy statutes" (Psa. 119:71). We do not know to what period in David's life these passages have reference. Perhaps they refer to his sins with Bathsheba or other unrecorded circumstances in which he went "astray" and consequently brought God's affliction down upon his life. It is impressive that divine affliction resulted in David both keeping and learning God's Word. It has been exactly the same in my own life.

In October 1950, I was knocked unconscious in a football accident. I remember the aftermath as though it were yesterday. Flat on my back in Vanderbilt University Hospital, Nashville, Tennessee, Dr. Nevil Leffko stood over my bed and announced: "Young man, you will never walk again." My world and dreams were shattered by his blunt words. I recall grinding my teeth and flushing in deep anger at his words. Struggling in helpless despair I determined I would prove him wrong. For well over forty years since that grim pronunciation, I have not walked a single step without the aid of steel braces on both legs and crutches. The doctor was right. I was wrong. At the time of my accident, I had been saved some five years. Despite a deep longing in my heart to "know Christ and God," I had no one to teach or assist me in the things of Bible Christianity. So I did what was probably normal: I gradually drifted back into a life of sin and shame. The hunger to know more about the Christ who had gloriously saved my soul, was, oddly enough, never fully extinguished. But it was barely smoldering beneath the ashes of a wasted and confused teenage life.

Little did I realize or even understand that God had sent that football accident and the terrible suffering that followed, to rekindle the few dying coals of my conversion into a life-long fire of Christian missionary service. That devastating knock-out blow (as I made a head-on flying tackle) was in reality, God tackling me into a new vocation — into learning the true meaning of life and love and service. The deep and unspeakable adversity, frustration and despair that filled my young life during the years that followed were all to become part of my unique "vocare" from heaven.

A former star football quarterback and Golden Gloves boxer, I now faced the world and life as a miserable paraplegic! The prospects were indeed terrifying. Many were the dark thoughts that pounded at the door of my mind, demanding attention and action. Looking back, I was similar to weeping Jeremiah as he cried out: "I am a man that hath seen affliction by the rod of his wrath" (Lam. 3:1). But that "rod of (God's) wrath" had within its every stroke a secret but marvelous design, even to satisfy that long-time hunger and thirst to know the Christ that had saved my soul some years before. God, in His wisdom, kept His purposes hidden from me in those early years of my experience. I did not understand then, that it was the beginning of my life's calling from the Father's loving hand. A divine summons was handed to me that Friday night while laying unconscious on an American football field. And with it came the first shimmering rays of light, the light my soul had cried out for since the demise of the joy of my conversion experience. My sun was about to rise!

Only a lad of eighteen years old and bewildered in my frustrations, I looked upon "myself" as a helpless cripple, paralysed from my waist down! Now, looking back, I can understand the pitiful lament of Gideon as he bleated out his objection to God: "Oh my Lord, if the Lord be with us, why then is all this befallen us?" (Judges 6:13). However, at that time I did not understand that ". . . God meant it unto good" (Gen. 50:20). And that "God chooses the foolish things, the weak things, things that are abase and things that are not" through which to accomplish His purposes (I Cor. 1:26-28). I did not know the passage which declares that the

Almighty who lives in heaven above also looks " . . . even to him that is poor and of a contrite (or broken) spirit . . ." (Isa. 66:2). Self "Reproach had broken mine heart" (Psa. 69:20), but I was to learn in years to come that "The sacrifices of God are a broken spirit: a broken and a contrite heart . . ." (Psa. 51:17). I will long remember when it dawned upon me during a communion service that "broken bread" symbolized the body of my Savior (Matt. 26:26). I wondered if my brokenness could somehow reflect my wonderful Lord? If it would, I determined to try and cherish it all the days of my life. A beautiful intention, but difficult to fulfil.

Many years later while serving as a missionary church-planter in the desert regions of central Australia, I discovered the marvelous passages of Psalm 147:10-11: "He delighteth not in the strength of the horse: he taketh not pleasure IN THE LEGS OF A MAN. The Lord taketh pleasure in them that fear him, in those that hope in his mercy." I cannot express the joy that flooded my heart upon reading these words. The troubling verse of Hebrews 12:13, now for the first time made sense. It was explained to my heart. I could be God's delight! He was not looking for strong legs, but for a man to fear Him in love and hope in His mercy. My highest calling was beginning to be realized. It all started in that football accident, when God tackled me. In the decades that followed, I was to learn the closer we seek to follow the Master, the more we are led into the deeper meaning of the cross; into the very treasures of pain and hurting that have so twisted and distorted the human race. That which disfigures the unsaved is designed by the heavenly "vocare" to transform true Christians into "living letters" which thunder forth the testimony of God's saving grace to all who pause to read.

Chapter 8

From the Microphone to The Master

After completing the courses at radio announcers' college, I entered public life with a "sitting down job." After all, "a paraplegic can't do much," I was often told. Professional radio announcing would be a fitting career. From the football field, to months in the hospital, to the shameful agonies of "rehabilitation," to college and finally to my first job at the "mike," an unseen (and at that time unknown) nail-scarred hand overshadowed the whole process. Deep in my heart I remembered with joy and frustration my salvation, and the dear Sunday school teacher (Mrs. Ruth Gifford) who won me to Christ. Having never grown in grace, even one inch, I buried those puzzling memories as something of a failure on my part, and threw myself completely into my announcing career. College friends had reminded me that I must plan for myself and the future. Alas, little did I know that my kind heavenly Father had already laid all the necessary plans and was slowly moving my confused and troubled life towards their fulfillment. The first act was not far away.

Among my duties was "signing on the air" the clergymen of our city for the popular program known as the "Ministers' Hour" (even though they had only thirty minutes each). One of my colleagues had previously warned me about a local preacher who had taken religion too far. I was to sign him on and off the air "in two weeks" time. My German friend firmly suggested that I should not "become involved" with him. I courteously listened to this advice and returned to my duties, giving it no more thought. After signing the "fanatic" on the air, I moved into the newsroom to clear the teletype machine, collecting the bulletins for the popular noon time news. I suddenly caught myself listening imperceptibly, as the pastor's message was relayed through the overhead speaker. He was preaching about the parable of the sower (Matt. 13:1-9). His potent words penetrated my soul like a knife: "God's message falls upon human hearts, but all do not receive it." Despite my abysmal lack of Bible knowledge, I knew, then and there, this was truth! And I knew that God's Word had fallen into my poor heart years before when I was saved; alas, what had I done with it? I was so mightily convicted that the old teletype machine piled paper on top of my shoes without my realizing it, until I tried to get back to the control room and stumbled against the door. My real vocation was drawing near. Something happened inside me that morning and it uncovered the buried memories of my conversion that Sunday in years gone by. The grace of God was slowly turning my heart towards my heavenly "vocare."

One month later, I found myself sitting in the very back row of the same minister's church. It was the Sunday evening service. Several hundred people literally packed the place out. I was deeply touched by the sweet and powerful singing. Then the pastor of whom I had been warned stood to preach. His text is still fresh in my mind. Reading from Matthew 9:36-38, he preached the most stirring sermon I had ever heard in my life. I can almost hear him now as I type these words: "Has God called you to the harvest field?" And, "Never forget, God has a plan and purpose for your life, regardless of who you are." Again it registered as truth to my weary soul. At the conclusion of the meeting, I somehow managed to stumble to the front. Literally dropping into a large pulpit chair, I told the concerned minister: "O, help me find my way back to God!" He did just that. Returning to my room that night, I felt fresh and clean on the inside, as I had at my conversion. Little did I know but a whole new world and life was about to dawn upon the little crippled radio announcer. And it did in the wee hours of the next morning.

According to the work schedule it was my duty to sign the station on the air. Pulling my lifeless legs up the thirty-one stairs to the second floor of the Bell Building, I glanced at my watch and noticed it was 4 a.m. The sun was not yet up. The darkness of the long hallway sent something of a chill over my shoulders as I unlocked the door and entered the control room. But that morning it was all different. Foremost in my mind was my effort to "find God anew" in that church service. A heavenly serenade of inward peace sounded sweet music throughout my soul. Getting things ready to begin the day's transmission I saw from the big clock on the wall, that I had yet another thirty minutes. Almost as if it were a normal and natural habit, I gently slid from the big announcer's chair and bowed down on my steel-embraced knees to the floor of the control room. I felt totally "at home" in the posture of prayer! My words went something like this: "O God, I don't know anything about this, but if you can use my life, I want to give it to you now." Somehow, I imagine, everyone in heaven must have stopped a moment to behold that amazing scene and listen to those simple but sincere words; anyway, I now know that God heard them. About five months later, I surrendered my life to preach the unsearchable riches of Christ. I had taken the first step toward my calling, my vocation. Over the next forty years, I was to tremblingly enter into the experience of taking up the cross and following Christ (Matt. 10:38). God would teach me that not all of life's roses smell good; only a few. But these few are worth the fight.

The grace of God had transported me from the microphone to the Master. Now for the rest of my life I had something wonderfully new to announce to all who would listen. It was the Good News of the saving Gospel of Christ; a message of hope, love, forgiveness and eternal life for all who would repent and believe.

Oddly enough, (like Jacob's son, Asher), I have lived and served God within the same divine sentence: "Thy shoes shall be iron and brass . . ." (Deut. 33:25). As these words are typed, my withered, impotent feet bear "shoes of iron and brass", and have done so for over four decades. Wonderful, "vocare" from God. Yet, strange and mystic, even defying all sensible logic and reasoning. Our hope in Christ is so profound, that it is beyond human conclusions. For me, it is a curious but delightful paradox when Holy Scripture declares: "How beautiful are the feet of them that

41

preach the gospel of peace, and bring glad tidings of good things" (Rom. 10:15). What a marvel, that even paraplegic feet are counted "beautiful" if they are ". . . shod with the preparation of the gospel of peace" (Eph. 6:15).

My journey from the microphone to the Master was a triumph of God's grace in the despair and ruin of a young human life. Yours can be the same! (See Chapter 19.)

Chapter 9

————≫••◦◦●◉●◦◦••◦≪————

Which View? From the Bottom or the Top?

While passing through this world we always examine our experiences and problems from the bottom side up. God's view however, is better. He sees them from the top side down! That perspective accommodates total understanding and makes possible a view of how all things will consummate into His final and eternal glory. So often, even with Bible in hand, and with its ". . . exceeding great and precious promises" (II Peter 1:3), we wail with Jeremiah: "Woe is me now! for the Lord hath added grief to my sorrow; I fainted in my sighing, and I find no rest" (Jer. 45:3). And this He does, but always for our good. Trying to maintain a loving trust in our Lord, we struggle hard with our sorrows and sufferings lest they swallow us up. Sometimes they do! In these times we feel like Jerusalem of which it was written: ". . . she had no comforter" (Lam. 1:9).

Some years after David had miraculously killed the terrifying Goliath, he fell into another war. Again it was with the dreaded Philistines. We are shocked and greatly dismayed to read his reaction in this battle: ". . . and David waxed faint" (II Sam. 21:15). How could such a thing ever be? The answer is simple: David's experience with Goliath did not make him an invincible believer. Years after the battle with the giant, he was still David! Within our calling from God, we too, like Jeremiah find "grief added to our sorrow" or the victory of a former battle not sufficient for a present one. Our Lord may see it good to change our company of fellowship into that of Job: "I am a brother to dragons, and a companion to owls" (Job 30:29). In such times it becomes God's glory for us to bear all these tough experiences for his honor and our self discipline. Ultimately, it all has a glorious objective. But alas! how many times have we missed this truth? Even Jesus crying from the humanity of His flesh, while hanging on the cross questioned: "My God, my God, why hast thou forsaken me . . .?" (Psa. 22:1).

Amid the rattle and clamor of a world going mad in sin and disobedience to God we must be continually disciplined to keep in mind our vocation. We share in a mysterious way the experiences of Christ in the body of His flesh. Contemplating the approaching death of the cross and its unspeakable "baptism of suffering" (Matt. 10:22,23), our Lord interrogated His confused disciples with a piercing statement: ". . . the cup which my Father hath given me, shall I not drink of it?" (John 18:11). The next morning the Lord Jesus drank the full cup of Calvary's sufferings and agony as He died for our sins. Later on, most of those very disciples also drank their cups as they suffered for the cause and glory of their Lord.

Every obedient Christian, walking in fellowship with his Savior, in similar fashion is given many strange cups to drink from the Father in Heaven. Shall we not (also) drink them? Not infrequently our cups will be large and deep and their contents will taste as the bitterness of wormwood. Christ went all the way: shall we do less? But even our Lord often faced a fierce struggle in the flesh of His incarnation. We read: "My soul is exceeding sorrowful unto death . . . " and "Abba, Father, all things are possible unto thee; take away this cup from me: nevertheless not what I will, but what thou wilt" (Mark 14:34,36). This struggle, pleading and final submission in prayer, mirrors all of us. Paul wrote: ". . . the sufferings of Christ abound in us" (II Cor. 1:5). Do they abound in you? Or, are you guilty of trying to explain them away by a cheap, vulgar approach to such Scriptures? Super faith does not always deliver the Christian from such experiences; rather it continually brings him into them. God will hand you numerous cups. Often their contents will be almost unbearable or unthinkable. It is part of our "vocare" to drink long, deep and frequent draughts from each one. The hand that passes them down to us is the hand that was nailed to the cross. It may be totally trusted.

In many years of foreign missionary service, I have often felt

44

as Christ when He cried out His sufferings through the pen of the Psalmist: "Reproach hath filled my heart; and I am full of heaviness: and I looked for some to take pity, but there was none; and for comforters, but I found none" (Psa. 69:20). Even like ". . . a sparrow alone upon the house top" (Psa. 102:7), so many times, I have, in frustration, failed to grasp the promise of Matthew 28:20: ". . . I am with you always, even unto the end of the world," and therefore cheated myself out of the consolation and strength such promises can give. Too often have I looked from the bottom side up, the bad view. God's "vocare" upon individual lives will bring us to ". . . lien among pots" (a darkened junk-room for dried dung and broken instruments) only to finally bring us out ". . . as the wings of a dove covered with silver, and her feathers of yellow gold" (Psa. 68:13). In His infinite wisdom, God sees fit to lead us over such paths and, like the ancient potter, to reshape and form anew each vessel ". . . as seemed good" to Himself (Jer. 18:1-6). All because He views our lives from the top side down and knows their ultimate end.

Extremists and angry readers will quickly interpret these words as unalterable declarations of doom or pessimism. God has not programmed our lives in this direction. What He has chosen is only the best, for ". . . shall not the judge of all the earth do right?" (Gen. 18:25). "For I know the thoughts that I think toward you, saith the Lord, thoughts of peace, and not of evil, to give you an expected end" (Jer. 29:11). As surely as the hairs of our heads are numbered (Matt. 10:30) and ". . . neither death, nor life, nor angels, nor principalities, nor powers, nor things present, nor things to come, nor height, nor depth, nor any other creature shall be able to separate us from the love of God . . ." (Rom. 8:38-39), God's jealous care abides over His own. "The Lord is righteous in all His ways" (Psa. 145:17). A mind broken by woe and distress may very well read "doom" into life's cups of whatever content. Meanwhile God's steady hand is on the wheel.

Missionary Paul mostly had the correct insight into his sufferings and woes. He speaks as a conquering monarch: "Who shall separate us from the love of Christ? shall tribulation, or

45

distress, or persecution, or famine, or nakedness, or peril, or sword?" (Rom. 8:35). We should remember that this is the Christian preacher who said of himself: "For thy (Christ's) sake we are killed all the day long; we are accounted as sheep for the slaughter" (Rom. 8:36). To be "killed all the day long" was Paul's assignment from the Lord. Our own cannot be much different. "Sheep for the slaughter" is not a very attractive prospect. The expression "killed all the day long" reflects lifelong suffering in the service of Christ. This is the normal Christian life; the believer's "Moriah" (Gen. 22:1-9) for knife and sacrifice. And like Abraham it will consummate into our eternal good and His everlasting glory. What a marvelous "vocare" we have from the hand of our loving Lord.

Those familiar with church history may remember that among early believers, some were inflamed or obsessed with a desire to be martyred for their faith. This passion for suffering and death was almost a psychological disorder as one can detect from reading their works. I do not speak of such self-imposed suffering for Christ, but only of God's divine will for His children. Not what the foolish vanity of man brings upon himself.

Even though Christians are comparable to sheep slaughtered daily, dauntless Paul still instructed his beloved converts to "Rejoice in the Lord alway: again I say rejoice" (Phil. 4:4). The "vocare" of God upon the life of every saved, dedicated, obedient believer is ". . . sorrowful, yet always rejoicing . . ." (II Cor. 6:10). Only the all-wise One could blend such distinct opposites as sorrow and joy to produce harmony in a man's heart. Our sorrow is not ". . . the sorrow of the world (which) worketh death" (II Cor. 7:10). Neither is it the sorrow of those who ". . . have no hope" (I Thess. 4:13). Christ described the sufferings of His children in these beautiful words: "Verily, verily, I say unto you, That ye shall weep and lament, but the world shall rejoice: and ye shall be sorrowful, but your sorrow shall be turned into joy . . . And now therefore ye have sorrow: but I will see you again, and your heart shall rejoice, and your joy no man taketh from you" (John 16:20,22). Our faithful Lord is watching earth's events from the top side down; He is directing our lives, assigning our work to fulfil the "vocare" given to each believer. Our admonition is to ". . . run with patience the race that is set before us" (Heb. 12:1). And in the discipline of perseverance, we are called upon to ". . . bear the burden and heat of the day" (Matt. 20:12). At times, suffering's long hour seems to never end. But it will.

A word of caution is necessary. Because our Lord has appointed us to this manner of earthly life and seen fit to include suffering, sorrow, pain and finally death as part of our ministry, does not mean we are to shun help, consolation, medication and relief. Such reasoning is nothing but buffoonery; it would condemn suffering Christians to a prison of inescapable, meaningless misery. In the face of my own physical pain, I have diligently sought medical relief. God sends the rain as a necessary blessing, but we use umbrellas and roofs to keep it off our heads. This does not signal that we reject what God is sending from heaven, but rather that we seek to receive the rains in common sense measure according to our needs.

In 1966, while conducting meetings in Houston, Texas, a "no doctor, no medicine, no-get-sick" charismatic preacher harangued me with this question: "If you believe God lets you get sick and suffer, then why do you go to the doctor?" I quietly replied to his obvious chicanery: "God lets darkness cover the earth at sundown, but I turn my electric lights on anyhow. According to your reasoning, I am to sit in darkness, because God caused it." Later, as this man was leaving the church office, I bade him farewell with this challenge: "Remember, don't ever turn your lights on when it's dark and I'll never go to the doctor when I'm sick. Is it a deal?" The only reply I received was a puzzling half-smile. I purposely tailored my answer to comply with the instruction of Proverbs 26:5: "Answer a fool according to his folly, lest he be wise in his own conceit." Those who follow the absurd logic of this zealous pastor are rejecting what physical comfort and relief one may find in life (see Prov. 17:22; Jer. 30:13; Matt. 9:12 and Mark 6:31). Years later, while again on furlough, I learned that this minister died a "horrible death of suffering" as a result of terminal cancer.

47

Incidentally, he did go to the doctor and hospital. It is curious how God makes us eat our famous words. I have become rather professional at this.

That poor man was stuck in his denomination's theological mud hole. It was reflected in his argument "God LETS you get sick." In these words we again encounter the nonsense of holding God responsible for our own irresponsibilities. Some of us simply get sick due to our silly negligence and not because God always drops it on our heads. The best view of our sufferings and sorrows is the heavenly one. To inspect them from the human side upward is disheartening at the best of times.

Chapter 10

The Fruits of Suffering: Taunting the Fire

Though much of my life and ministry has been attended by suffering and sorrow, it is not yet over. I suspect God may yet have more for me to experience and endure. The final objectives can be numerous: to burn out the bad and bring in the good, to purify, purge, cleanse, to lift one's aspirations and ideals onto a level high above that of a blinded world (see Job 23:10), to give holy insights, wisdom, understanding — to open one's eyes to truly see. I see better, clearer, purer when my eyes stream with tears, even though, at such times, I often fail to see my Lord. Before the foundation of the world, God Almighty predestined (set out before hand) that His own beloved children should be conformed "to the image of His Son" (Rom. 8:29). The main instrument through which He performs this lifelong work is suffering. It is part of our calling, of our "vocare."

Peter reminds us of another purpose of the heartache and woe through which believers frequently pass: "That the trial of your faith, being much more precious than of gold that perisheth, though it be tried with fire, might be found unto praise and honor and glory at the appearing of Jesus Christ" (I Peter 1:7). A tried faith that stands under the pressure and heat will be faith of "praise and honor and glory" in the presence of our wonderful Lord! Romans puts it like this: "But glory, honor, and peace, to every man that worketh good . . . " (Rom. 2:10). In harmony with Romans 5:3 (previously mentioned), James writes: "Knowing this, that the trying of your faith worketh patience" (Jam. 1:3). Suffering endured for Christ's sake carries millennial benefit: "If we suffer, we shall also reign with Him . . ." (II Tim. 2:12).

I look about on every side, but fail to see that ". . . glorious church, not having spot, or wrinkle, or any such thing . . . " (Eph. 5:27). The closest approximation that I have found were the Christians behind the former Iron Curtain. But even they had their "spots, wrinkles and sins." The portion of Christ's church that has attained this pure consummation are those who have suffered their final heartache, and now rest at Jesus' feet (Heb. 12:22-23). Some of us are not very far from joining them. Only when God's plan for earth and man is completed will we see that beautiful bride, that church of Ephesians 5:26-27. In the interim, we are on the stage of life's drama, acting out our parts. Through the supply of God's grace we accept our heavenly "vocares," the nail-scarred hands directing the course He has wisely charted. Seeking to be ". . . joyful in all our tribulation . . ." (II Cor. 7:4), we are slowly learning to ". . . always triumph in Christ" (II Cor. 2:14), how to " . . . sit together in heavenly places in Christ Jesus . . . " (Eph. 2:6). Great faith is manifested not so much in public display to do, as in secret ability to suffer. Within these awful confines, God is preparing a people in whom He "taketh pleasure" (Psa. 149:4).

Even though the sufferings and trials of our calling often cut deep, we must disdain to borrow sorrow from tomorrow. Veteran followers of the Lamb refuse to take out an advanced loan on next month's troubles, for "Sufficient unto the day is the evil thereof" (Matt. 6:34). The dayspring (Lk 1:78) from on high keeps reminding us that "He shall choose our inheritance . . ." (Psa. 47:4). If this "inheritance" calls some to Moses' depressing loneliness on "the backside of the desert" (Ex. 3:1), to Aaron's choking silence upon the death of his wicked sons (Lev. 10:6), to Naomi's distress at the loss of her family (Ruth 1:21), to David's threats from a godless father-in-law (I Sam. 19:1), to Elijah's hideout "by the brook Cherith" (I Kings 17:4), to Job's cursings (Job 3:1-10), to Isaiah's shame (Isa. 20), to Jeremiah's dungeon (Jer. 38:6), to Hosea's humiliation (Hos. 1:2-3), to Joseph's dilemma (Matt. 1:18-19), to Jesus' disappointment (Matt. 26:40), to Paul's fears at Corinth (Acts 18:9) or to John's confrontation with Diotrephes (III John 9-10), we may be sure that "God meant it unto good" (Gen.

50:20).

Because this is true, in whatever life may bring we have God's Word of good cheer: "When thou passest through the waters, I will be with thee; and through the rivers, they shall not overflow thee: when thou walkest through the fire thou shalt not be burned: neither shall the flame kindle upon thee" (Isa. 43:2). Therefore, with Godly sarcasm, even holy satire, we tease the flames that have wounded and purged us again and again and for so many years. Our joyful taunt is: "Aha, I am warm, I have seen the fire" (Isa. 44:16). Again it was for our good and His glory. It was even sent from heaven with love.

Ancient Hebrew pilgrims, faced with the wearying journey, often involving hundreds of miles, to Jerusalem's temple to keep their annual feasts, would paint the name of Jehovah God (in tetragrammation) upon the palms of their hands. A hundred times a day their eyes would fall upon this beloved name; their spirits were refreshed. God tells His weary children in Isaiah's day: "Behold, I have graven thee upon the palms of my hands" (Isa. 49:16). He sees us in our struggles. Your name is on His powerful but tender hands. Speaking of taunting the fire: It is indeed both sobering and humorous that many of the things which make us weep and miserable today, we can laugh at tomorrow.

Chapter 11

———•••✦◆✦•••———

The Fellowship of His Sufferings

For years I have been attracted to, but disturbed by, the words of Paul in Philippians 3:10. Speaking of the Savior, he writes: "That I may know Him, and the power of His resurrection and the fellowship of His sufferings, being made conformable (or like) unto His death." I sincerely enjoy proper Christian fellowship; but, even more greatly do I enjoy my hours alone with God and His Word. "Fellowship" comes from a root word meaning "a sharer." It is at this very point that I have been left in wonder. How could Paul ever long to be "a sharer" in the sufferings of Christ? Frankly, I have had enough of hurting and pain. Yet, I am clearly seeing it as part of my life's work, part of my ministry and calling from God. Our ministries must be completed. Paul wrote to a friend: "Take heed to the ministry which thou has received in the Lord, that thou fulfil it" (Col. 4:17). He practiced what he preached. At the end of his "vocare," in the death cell of a Roman prison, he pens this triumphant eulogy: "For I am now ready to be offered, and the time of my departure is at hand. I have fought a good fight, I have finished my course, I have kept the faith" (II Tim. 4:6-7).

To contemplate physically sharing in the sufferings of our Lord is beyond comprehension. No human ever suffered as Christ. None of His sufferings were His own! He was history's only sinless man. He ". . . did no sin, neither was guile found in his mouth" (I Peter 2:22). Every sorrow, pain, grief, hurt, heartache, oppression, disappointment, agony, confusion, frustration, even sickness and infirmity that Christ bore, belonged to someone else: to you and me. It is impossible to try to grasp the theological depth of passages that declare that all of our sins were laid on Christ, or that He bore our sicknesses, or that He (Who knew no sin) was made sin for us, or that God laid on Him the iniquity of us all (see Isa. 53:3-7, 10; Matt. 8:17; Lk 22:44; John 11:33; II Cor. 5:21; Heb. 5:7 and I Peter 1:18-20). If I think of my own sins, I am overwhelmed. But, to think that Jesus Christ took and carried all the sins of all men, of all times, and then was killed by God, as the judgment on these sins, is simply too much. The unspeakable evil, wickedness, filth, vice, corruption, the perversions, the brokenness of humanity, the tears, sighs, cries and groans of the lost race of Adam — Christ had ALL laid on Him! Who in his right mind would seek to share in such abhorrent and appalling experiences? The text says Missionary Paul did. And we are called into the same fellowship, each according to his place and purpose in Christian service and ministry.

Never can this be interpreted to mean that Christians, as it were, take into their bodies the sins of lost mankind. We would go completely insane under such a load. Every Christian would be consigned to a straightjacket and a padded cell. Paul is not speaking of fellowship with Christ in His literal, vicarious, expiatory sufferings, paying the price for the atonement of sins. Rather, he craves to share more deeply in the "offense of the cross," the daily martyrdom for living and preaching the truth of God, the "deaths often" of his missionary life. The very true and real sufferings which were part of winning, helping and loving lost men for Christ's sake.

Read this great man's graphic description, filled with deep pathos, as he writes to his Corinthian church: "For I think that God hath set forth us the apostles last, as it were appointed to death: for we are made a spectacle unto the world, and to angels and to men. We are fools for Christ's sake, but ye are wise in Christ; we are weak, but ye are strong; ye are honorable, but we are despised. Even unto this present hour we both hunger, and thirst, and are naked, and are buffeted, and have no certain dwelling place; And labor, working with our hands: being reviled we bless; being persecuted we suffer it: Being defamed, we intreat: we are made as the filth of this world, and are the offscouring of all things unto this day" (I Cor. 4:9-13). Here we have a chilling but glorious panorama of his missionary life. Also deep insight into his earthly "vocare."

Few today would agonize before God in prayer, asking for the "fellowship of His sufferings" to become part of their experience and calling. Surely none of us can fully emulate Paul's extraordinary life. Yet every saved, called, dedicated saint has (like Paul) the appointment of Philippians 1:29 stamped upon his life: "For unto you it is given in the behalf of Christ, not only to believe on Him, but also to suffer for His sake." Paul wrote to the church at Colosse these amazing words: "(I) now rejoice in my sufferings for you, and fill up that which is behind of the afflictions of Christ in my flesh . . . " (Col. 1:24). Such words cannot be understood to mean, that he was somehow trying to complete, or add something, to the sufferings of Christ (for our sins) to make atonement thorough and absolute. He had fellowship in the sufferings of Jesus only as he gave his life in the Master's service. This missionary knew that the end of all Christian suffering finds its meaning in God.

The concept that our suffering completes atonement is dogmatized by the Roman Catholic church. It teaches that the merits, deeds and sufferings of the saints are added to the sufferings of Christ on the cross. Together, they make forgiveness and atonement absolute. Such doctrine is a masterpiece of blasphemy. As in Philippians 3:10, Paul is rejoicing that he has been called to suffer (as all believers have been) for the sake of God's truth and righteousness. Not to play some part in his personal salvation.

Psalm 88 was penned by the Hebrew musician and song leader, Heman. In ancient Jewish poetry it is usually called a "Song of Distress." The eighteen verses of this peculiar Psalm tremble with the themes of suffering, distress and sorrow. Some old wise man said that every child of God must, over the course of life, walk through all of these eighteen verses. For the Lord leads us in this way. It speaks of distress of "unanswered prayers" (verses 1-2), of "many troubles" (verse 3), of "wishing even to die" (verses 4-5), of "being in darkness and feeling cut off from God" (verse 6), of "suffering many afflictions and sinking in the depths of despair" (verse 7), of "estrangement from friends" (verse 8), of "mourning" (verse 9), and of "sorrows from youthful days upward" (verse 15). Who would believe that God directed Heman along such paths? I do. I have travelled many of these myself. I can relate to this song of the Hebrew lyricist. Perhaps God is even trying to teach us to sing it along the pathway of life?

The Lord has ordained that we partake in this mystical and often difficult fellowship of sufferings. The hurt we experience in this fellowship is for our benefit, never our harm. A rose, however beautiful, cannot release its pleasing, alluring fragrance until it has been broken and crushed. Then the rose does its supreme work. In Bible lands, the fierce, thrashing north and south winds sweep continually through the gardens of tender, beautiful flowers. The husbandman purposefully planted them so that they would receive the wind's full fury! Of this, Solomon writes: "Awake, o north wind; and come, thou south; blow upon my garden, that the spices thereof may flow out" (Song of Sol. 4:16). Only as the crosswinds buffet the flowers can the matchless odor of heavenly sweetness flow out. It is the same with God's children in every age.

We have the "vocare" to be buffeted by the winds of adversity, sorrow, trials and sufferings. Because of these beatings the heavenly perfume of our Savior flows from our brokenness to "fill the house," then, others may profit (John 12:3). It is only when we are thus exposed that we can understand the meaning of Proverbs 10:22: "The blessing of the Lord, it maketh rich, and he addeth no sorrow with it." Out of such experiences flow genuine blessing and true richness. Sadly, not many of God's children seem to attain the disciplined mind from which this view can be appreciated. The whole of human nature with its complete depravity and vileness rises in fierce opposition to the theology of the fellowship of Christ's sufferings.

Within the camp of certain Christians we frequently hear several of those who dote themselves "Reformed," decrying such Bible truths and historically proven facts as being "Antinomianism" or "Arminianism. The pseudo-grace they have invented carries with it (so they tell us) the automatic compulsion for the saved to always do right. This, then, becomes the source of their sanctified living. It allows no place for the true saving grace of God to prove itself over and over in the daily lives of His struggling children, and thereby demonstrate the divine perseverance of the saints. Genuine sovereign grace, present, active, objective and sufficient does. In some cases, perhaps, "Deformed" should be substituted for "Reformed." It's more descriptive and honest.

Beware of any theology that plays down or scorns the fellowship of our Lord's sufferings. Truly, it may spring from sincerity, but deeper, it is not from God. Fervent sincerity, not balanced and motivated by truth, is one of this world's greatest evils (I Cor. 5:8).

Chapter 12

Interpreting Life Right

Occasionally I am rebuked into deep shame while reflecting upon the life of Paul and other saints of the Bible. Most of the time, they had the spiritual insight, a gift of discernment, the rare ability to interpret the unannounced calamities impinging on their lives as, ultimately, having a divine design. (For the believer who is knowingly living in sin and in wilful disobedience and who refuses to follow on with Christ, this may not be so.)

Writing to the Philippian assembly, some six years after departing from them, Paul calls to remembrance the sufferings he endured while preaching in that Roman colony: "But I would ye should understand brethren, that the things which happened unto me have fallen out rather unto the furtherance of the Gospel" (Phil. 1:12 with I Thess. 2:2). One of the "shameful things" that the apostle endured was being stripped and beaten publicly (see Acts 16:22-23). I am sure that during the painful beating Paul saw little, if anything of God. When Dr. Leffko told me I would "never walk again," I can promise you that, in my mind, God was nowhere to be found. In 1989, I was facing death in the Royal Brisbane Hospital in Australia, due to kidney failure, and suffering to the end of human endurance. I could not find God in the long ordeal. When my wife and I received a long-distance telephone call at midnight on September 27, 1989, informing us that our thirty-three-year-old son had been given approximately eight weeks to live on account of terminal cancer, frankly for a few days I could barely remember God even existed. Our minds were stunned. We were reduced to a zombie-like state. When one of the dearest pastor friends I ever had fell into gross sin, for several weeks I lived and moved in a dazed condition. Inwardly, I felt an affinity with the Psalmist: ". . . my spirit was overwhelmed within me . . ." (Psa. 142:3). So often with David I have knelt in the burnt-out ashes of another of my life's Ziklags, but unlike him, on these occasions, I often failed to ". . . encourage (myself) in the Lord (my) God." (See I Sam. 30:1 and 6 for the meaning of Ziklag).

Frequently we become so swallowed up in griefs and sorrows, that for the moment, we let slip the sure promise of God that He is ". . . not far from every one of us" (Acts 17:27), or "The Lord is at hand" (Phil. 4:5). It is possible to be so overwhelmed by some of life's fierce storms that our hearts faint and succumb under the crushing load. Like the children of Israel, to whom God sent Moses to preach the message of new hope and deliverance from the sufferings of Egypt, we read: ". . . but they hearkened not unto Moses for anguish of spirit, and for cruel bondage" (Ex. 6:9). I am not a super, iron-man Christian. Many times I have felt as those Jews in Egypt; when anguish was so deep, I too could not hear the message of God for my life. I have walked in the meanings of Proverbs 12:25: "Heaviness in the heart of man maketh it stoop"; and Proverbs 14:13: "Even in laughter the heart is sorrowful . . . ." Further, I have experienced the truth of Proverbs 18:14: ". . . a wounded spirit who can bear?" But it was all from my side. I was temporarily dead to the life-giving message of God. My prayers seemed to mock me as I cried with Christ from His cross of suffering: ". . . why art thou so far from helping me, and from the words of my roaring" (Psa. 22:1). A tidal wave of sorrow had deafened my ears to the gentle voice of Jesus: "Why are ye so fearful? How is it that ye have no faith?" (Mk 4:40). Apparently, most of the time Paul was not given to such defeats. He usually had the discipline and spiritual discernment to interpret life's storms aright.

Looking back on his sufferings at Philippi, some six years later, Paul then understood they had fallen out for the furtherance (speeding on) of the Gospel (Phil. 1:12). God used a public beating in nakedness and shame for the salvation of the city jail-keeper and his whole family (Acts 16:24-34). "Surely the wrath of man shall praise thee" (Psa. 76:10), would be Asaph's comment on Paul's beating. And even while writing the Philippian letter Paul was sitting under house arrest in Rome, Italy (Acts 28:16, 30-31). Yet, he had the spiritual discernment to interpret God into this whole experience. He was always "a prisoner of Christ" never of Rome (Eph. 3:1; 4:1). His sufferings had fired a new courage into the faint hearts of weaker missionaries and preachers; his bonds (chains) had given them this much-needed impetus and valor. Listen to Paul's summation: "So that my bonds in Christ are manifest in all the palace (the law court of Rome and the soldiers' barracks) and in all other places" (Phil. 1:13). I have wondered how many ex-Roman soldiers will be in heaven with me because Paul was subjected to house arrest and prison so frequently. Possibly a Roman governor (Acts 24:22, 24-26), or even a Caesar (see Acts 9:15 with 23:11 and 27:24) will be there.

The apostle's ability to interpret his life's sufferings aright are beautifully demonstrated in his classic words: ". . . I die daily" (I Cor. 15:31) and that he experienced ". . . deaths oft" (II Cor. 11:23). The greatly assorted strokes of pain and sorrow that fell upon his head were put into a divine context: "For we which live are always delivered unto death for Jesus' sake, that the life of Jesus might be made manifest in our mortal flesh. So then death worketh in us . . ." (II Cor. 4:11-12). Paul tasted of death daily, in order that he might through these deaths demonstrate the true life of Christ to others. Couched in these words is a secret to understanding and living the true Christian life.

At the conclusion of his third missionary journey, Paul (through a secretary) writes the Epistle to the Romans (Rom. 16:22-24). This book is the pinnacle of Christian theology, the greatest masterpiece of divine doctrine, the very foundation of instruction for God's church. We detect in its pages that time and experience had seasoned Paul's understanding. Now he knows a few of the reasons "why?" and has learned from his suffering: ". . . knowing that tribulation worketh patience; And patience, experience; and experience hope: And hope maketh not ashamed . . ." (Rom 5:3-5). This veteran missionary looks back over the years and now understands the origin of patience and the fruit of it. Tribulation is the mother of patience. It will never be gained any other way. Only through "tribulations" will we develop the hope that maketh not ashamed. Perhaps we could say, "no hurt" means "no hope." Possibly, no heaven!

Is the main reason so many Christians are ashamed of their Savior and His Gospel, simply that they have not suffered for them? No wonder, early in the Roman letter Paul could write: "For I am not ashamed of the Gospel of Christ . . ." (verse 16). He reminded the Galatian believers that he bore in his physical body ". . . the marks of the Lord Jesus" (Gal. 6:17). Paul interpreted his continual sufferings aright and they had been endured over many years of faithful missionary service. Comparing them with the everlasting joys of heaven, he could write: "For our light affliction, which is but for a moment, worketh for us a far more exceeding and eternal weight of glory" (II Cor. 4:16).

Writing Timothy a final letter, the apostle records for his "son in the faith" some things to remember. Even with the shadow of death hovering over his head, Paul meditates on his newest sorrows: ". . . all they which are in Asia be turned away from me" (II Tim. 1:15) and "Demas" had forsaken him (II Tim. 4:10). Though it had been well over twenty years ago, he still remembers the "Persecutions, affliction, which came unto (him) at Antioch, at Iconium, at Lystra . . ." and that he "endured" them all (II Tim. 3:11). He solemnly warns Timothy to ". . . endure hardness as a good soldier of Jesus Christ" (II Tim. 2:3), and that all who will ". . . live Godly in Christ Jesus shall suffer persecution" (II Tim. 3:12). The aged missionary's final warning to his dearest friend rings like a rifle shot: "But watch thou in all things, endure afflictions . . ." (II Tim. 4:5). Continually, Paul warned converts, friends and churches with these sobering words: "That no man should be moved by these afflictions: for yourselves know that we are appointed thereunto" (I Thess. 3:3). Knowing that he had been "appointed to suffer afflictions" and refusing to let them "move him," Paul was able to interpret Christian life and service correctly. From the time of his conversion on the Damascus road to his life's end (about 34 years later) his life was crowned with suffering and affliction for Christ's sake. Through it all he rejoiced in the prize set before him (II Tim. 4:18). Paul's "vocare" was now thoroughly understood and accepted with joy. He knew no tragedy could separate him from God's love.

We delight to quote Romans 8:28 for the benefit of fellow believers who are laboring under great distress or physical suffering. It's another story to quote it to yourself! If we are trying to live a dedicated life for our God, with confidence we may apply this verse in every situation. Even the sudden and earth-shaking experiences that crash upon us are embraced by this passage from God's Word. (If most readers are like me, it will probably take them days to get their thinking aright after life's most devastating experiences. Then, one may begin to absorb Romans 8:28. It remains true that we may be so beaten down, we need months or years to recover. Some of the scars we will carry to our graves.)

Rethinking some of my life, I now clearly see that my children would probably never have been saved, or my oldest grandchildren, or thousands of lost souls in America, Australia, South Africa and other places, had God not tackled me in that football game so many years ago. Out of that "tragic accident" (so my coach described it) has risen triumph in my life and in the lives of countless others. I think of a kind, elderly Italian Roman Catholic priest who, after three years of "talks," "discussions," "debates" and "secret meetings" with me, was finally saved. He later had to leave Australia. I remember the Presbyterian pastor of a church in (former) Rhodesia, converted in a Sunday evening meeting in front of his own church members! He was indeed a brave man. And there was the Baptist minister near Atlanta, Georgia, during our second furlough saved, to the joy of his wife.

Had God, in His foresight and providence, not arranged for me to be "fired because of my faith" from that radio station, and had I not subsequently found employment in a shoe heel factory, five fellow workers would probably be in hell today. They all came to Christ and passed away within the next thirty years. While serving at a small Bible School on the east coast of central

Queensland, Australia, our village grocery store proprietor fell ill with a terminal kidney disease. God impressed on my heart to fly some 1800 miles and search him out in a gigantic Brisbane hospital. At the end of one of the most grueling days of my life, walking some three city blocks on my crutches, with broken, bleeding blisters on both hands, I found my Chinese friend on his death bed. With a ward full of astonished, tough Australian men watching and listening, Ken Buhow was gloriously saved! Two months later he was in eternity. Another Romans 8:28! Had God not sent me into the Royal Brisbane Hospital suffering beyond description with kidney failure, Stanley Druse, a tough, hard-bitten Aussie cowboy, would not be in heaven today. He was saved and died of terminal cancer some fifteen months later. Had God not compelled me to linger late one evening in the dining hall of a small private hotel in the Black Forest of Germany, I would never have met the cook! Five nights later this young French woman, a member of the university branch of the Communist Party, was saved.

Never in living memory could my wife and I forget Bob Brodie. Bob was a cunning, mean, heavy drinking Aussie gambler. He was fierce with anger because his wife had been recently saved and baptized. In March 1963, a fellow Christian (Les West) who worked at the local Fire Department, tipped me off that rumors were spreading in the pubs that Bob was on his way to my house to "kill me," because his wife was now in the church. Deeply alarmed, I ordered my wife to lock herself and our small children into the bedroom as Bob pounded on our front door. Very reluctantly I invited him in! Half drunk, unshaven, a filthy, blood splattered white shirt, hanging out of his trousers, Bob dropped on the couch beside me. Setting in silence for some minutes he looked at the wall After mumbling some garbled few words and after a brief conversation, he snapped to his feet and stormed out. What a relief! The following Sunday night, he was wonderfully saved at the Faith Baptist Church, Gladstone, Queensland, Australia. For over 25 years this ex-gambler and notorious pub fighter, with his wife, Melva, have served the Christ who so greatly transformed their lives. God's wonderful grace changed Bob Brodie into a calm but fearless preacher of the saving Gospel and a dedicated servant of Christ. All this because God tackled me on that football field decades ago. As I edit these lines, this couple have entered into the worst storm of their lives. It will only be by God's sufficient grace and some good old fashion self discipline that they can ride this one out.

Space will not allow a full description of Helen Geddes (the daughter of a Swiss Reformed minister) mightily saved. In the years following, she has won hundreds of children to Jesus. Or Doug Allan, another Aussie gambler and big-time money man. My wife quoted a passage from Scripture to Doug (I Thess. 5:22), after he had courteously scorned her to justify his betting on the horses. Two years later that verse tracked him to a hospital bed, where he was converted to Christ. After two years of witnessing to the truck driver, Phil Brewster, he was saved and has preached God's Word ever since! His life has been torn by loss and suffering, but Philip has remained true to his Lord. This dear Christian man is a prime example of those who suffer horribly in this world created by God, yet love Him with all their hearts. There was also the staunch Roman Catholic, Kevin McMahon, down on his knees weeping his way to Calvary in Alice Springs, Australia. Kevin and Erica have served their Master for over 27 years among the Brethren Assemblies of Western Australia. (Erica was an unsaved Presbyterian. She came to Christ a few days following her husband's conversion.)

Ernie Hurst was a middle age, Australian truck driver. He lived in Alice Springs, Northern Territory. Late one Saturday afternoon, he phoned requesting that I "urgently" come to his house. Upon arrival, I saw him standing beside his yellow truck with both hands shoved deep into his pockets. Getting out of my car and locking both leg braces, I turned to greet Ernie. Suddenly he sprang forward, slammed me up against the car door and pushed a long knife toward my stomach! Sweating profusely, trembling and cursing violently, he shouted: "You Christians are all alike. I'm going to cut your guts out!" I can tell you I was terrified as I prayed from my heart for God's help. Then, amid the drama of it all, I noticed tears streaming down his sun burnt face. I reached forward. Placing my hand on his

65

shoulder and trying to be calm, I spoke softly: "Ernie what's wrong? Please let me help you." He broke into full tears and muttered the story. The local charismatic pastor had been visiting his wife, Hilda, who was seriously club-footed. He assured her of God's healing, if she would allow him to anoint her with oil and pray over her twisted feet. During her husband's absence at work, the minister entered the house and prayed for Mrs. Hurst. She was not healed, as promised. Now she was told, it was her fault because she "did not have faith in Jesus to do this miracle." Upon returning home, Ernie found his poor wife crushed, sinking in despair and weeping beyond control. Now he was ready to kill! He called me over and vented his frustration and wrath upon me. I asked him to look down at my legs and reminded him that they were in far worse condition than his wife's feet. And God had not healed me! He did, and fell upon my neck crying audibly. The knife dropped into the sand at my feet. A while later, we entered the house. I tried to console Hilda and point out the wickedness reflected in the dirty trick of the pastor who claimed the "gift of healing." Later that evening, in a pleasant atmosphere, I was able to lead Ernie to a saving knowledge of Christ. (Hilda had been previously saved.) Today, over twenty-nine years later, both Ernie and Hilda walk the streets of gold. Her feet are perfect. Soon, I shall see them again and we will all walk together over that wonderful place.

Traveling from Johannesburg to Port Elizabeth in South Africa, I stopped off half way amid the trip to preach in a Zulu college. The principal, Mr. Lubba, had previously arranged the meeting. Standing in the blistering sun for over one hour, the entire student body and staff listened with rapt attention as I spoke. There was no response at the conclusion of the service. I drove off to Port Elizabeth thinking nothing would come from the meeting. The following Monday, Mr. Lubba phoned me. I was informed that shortly after I drove away, the most promising male student in the college, meekly entered the principal's office. He requested to "be saved from hell"! The Godly principal led him to Christ. Saturday morning, this same young man went home to his village. While swimming in a pond late that same afternoon, he suddenly drowned!

This eighteen year old lad was "saved from hell" sooner than he thought.

Mrs. Crooks was a lovely, well dressed mother with three dear children and skeptic husband. She attended a meeting while I was preaching at the Bethany Baptist Church, near Pretoria, South Africa. At the end of the service she came into the pastor's study for prayer and counseling. Several others were present and experienced what was to follow. As I began to softly pray, she snapped into a frozen, iron-like, stiff posture on the couch where she was sitting. Her hands turned under, resembling animal claws; deep and horrible growls sounded from her throat as snow-white foam streamed down both sides of her mouth. The entire atmosphere of the pastor's study was filled with evil. Norman Balshaw, a good, trustworthy deacon looked at me in alarm and fear. This woman was demon possessed! After many exhausting hours of battle with evil spirits, screaming, swearing, accusing and speaking to us in (at least) five foreign languages (of which she had learned none), Mrs. Crooks was saved and mightily set free. It was one of the most enlightening experiences of my ministry and one of the most horrifying as well. (I can only relate portions of the story.) Over a year later I joyfully met both Mr. and Mrs. Crooks at a meeting in Durban, on the southern coast of South Africa. He too had been saved and both were walking in the praise and joy of the Lord. I will never forget the sheer glory that radiated from the dear woman's face — and no wonder!

I shall long remember being home on our third furlough. My sister phoned regarding our first cousin, James Barton. He was dying with terminal cancer. Driving to his home, I found him early one morning sitting at the kitchen table trembling under the ravages of that dreadful disease. Within five minutes, James, broken and weeping called on the Lord for eternal life. Two weeks later his body slept in the grave. His redeemed soul was resting in the presence of God. Never, can I forget my own dear father, saved at my ordination service. This is but a little of the fruit from a "vocare" of suffering, sickness and much pain. Looking back, I can see where Romans 8:28 happened to me numerous times. However, it has taken years for these wonderful events to come into clear focus. Oh the marvel of saving grace!

But it was not all glory and victory. Amid some of the vehement storms of my life I have failed God miserably. There was only void, darkness and confusion. Even prayer seemed to mock me for it was never answered. I could not find God (so I thought). The need was not supplied (as I understood it at the time). Nothing seemed right any more. I had to force myself to keep on believing in God! Without fail, however, as I finally emerged from each of these nightmare seasons, to my sheer delight, Jesus was there to greet me! Ashamedly, I learned He had been with me through it all, but placed His hand over my eyes so I could not see Him. But, in my frustration I cavilled with God. I had failed to embrace the grand promise of I Corinthians 10:13 thus forfeiting (in those dark times) its hope of a God-given way of escape. When thinking upon my miserable and wretched failures, I remember it is written: "For a just man falleth seven times, and riseth up again . . ." (Prov. 24:16).

Standing beside the bed of a terminally ill cancer patient at the Johannesburg General Hospital, I was softly reading to him the verses from II Timothy 3:10-12. Suddenly I saw it! Joyfully I read it over again. (This was for my profit not the sick man on his bed.) Paul was telling his friend Timothy: ". . . what persecutions I endured: but out of them all the Lord delivered me." There it was! God's Word says we are "delivered" from some things by "enduring" them! Who ever heard of deliverance by endurance? The Bible has! I can now see clearly that in my own life God has delivered me from many things by giving me the grace to endure them to the bitter end. It is untrue that our Lord will deliver us by some supernatural means from every earthquake that rips into our lives. Frequently He may use supernatural means, but many times He will not. We are delivered by enduring. Perhaps, we too must ". . . eat the fruit of our doings" (Isa. 3:10), and ". . . bear (our) burden" (Gal. 6:5). Like Jeremiah who cried out: "Woe is me for my hurt! my wound is grievous: but I said, Truly this is a grief, and I must bear it" (Jer. 10:19). Frankly, there are some things God

68

wants us to bear. He will not lift the load from our shoulders. Can this be the meaning of Lamentations 3:27? "It is good for a man that he bear the yoke in his youth."

All of this is still part of that "vocare" sent from God's heart to ours. It is Romans 8:28 flowering through and in these earthen vessels. "O the depth of the riches both of the wisdom and knowledge of God! how unsearchable are His judgments, and His ways past finding out!" (Rom. 11:33). Reflecting over the years gone by, I am better able to interpret life aright. Now I understand that most youthfulness is simply a form of temporary insanity, through which we must pass. Truly mid-life brings those years of maturity and amends-making; trying hard to put things right as they whisper to us from the years of life that are past. Seasoned by old age and the deepest love for Christ and fellowman, tempered by sufferings, with the thrills of life now over, we wait our final "vocare" — into the presence of God for ever!

Most of the things that befall us in this world will not be understood for the puzzling reason that God has determined it to be so. We read of this incomprehensible mystery in these difficult passages: "The secret things belong unto the Lord our God . . ." (Deut. 29:29), and in Proverbs 25:2: "It is the glory of God to conceal a thing . . . ." Theologians debate the question: Will God explain it all to us in heaven? Honestly, I do not know, nor do I care any more, for it will make no difference then. To those Christians who are right with God in their daily lives and are assailed by suffering, sorrow and often physical sickness, Peter gives instructions concerning what to do: "Wherefore let them that suffer according to the will of God commit the keeping of their souls to Him in well doing, as unto a faithful Creator" (I Peter 4:19).

Are you saved and in fellowship with God? Then begin now disciplining yourself to see the Lord's hand working, even in the bitter sorrows and deep disappointments of your Christian life. If your hopes, health and great plans for physical happiness crash about you, "commit the keeping of your (eternal) soul" to the One who has kept creation running for thousands of years. He can handle it quite well! Moses chose " . . . rather to suffer affliction with the people of God" and he "esteemed (considered) . . . the reproach of Christ greater riches than the treasures in Egypt" (Heb. 11:25-26). Who in their right mind would deliberately elect to suffer and bear reproach, in place of ease and shamelessness? God's informed, experienced and proven children, are however, learning this is part of their heavenly "vocare." Heaven leads its people to go this way as they follow the Lamb ". . . unto living fountains of waters: and God shall wipe away all tears from their eyes" (Rev. 7:17).

Our Lord is more interested in what we are gradually becoming through our trials and sufferings, than what we presently are. The ugly, repulsive caterpillar of today, through struggle and death, becomes the beautiful butterfly of tomorrow. "For I reckon that the sufferings of this present time are not worthy to be compared with the glory which shall be revealed in us" (Rom. 8:18).

Chapter 13

Thank You, God, for Everything?

Years ago, I heard a pastor speak on the first six words of II Corinthians 5:18: "And all things are of God . . . ." His introduction stunned me: "We are to praise and thank the Lord for everything; even evil, sin and Satan!" Included in the message were two other passages: "Giving thanks always for all things unto God" (Eph. 5:20) and "In everything give thanks for this is the will of God in Christ Jesus concerning you" (I Thess. 5:18). It must be noted that this verse reads: "IN everything give thanks" and not "FOR everything." There is a great difference. And the "for all things" in Ephesians 5:20, are clearly "unto God."

Unthankfulness is a detestable sin. Our Lord (who was God in human flesh) beautifully demonstrated thankfulness. Before feeding the masses from the little basket of fish and bread, He looked up toward heaven and gave thanks (Lk 9:16). Paul standing on the deck of a storm-battered ship, having not eaten in fourteen days, thanked God for his food (Acts 27:33-35), in the presence of insulting unbelievers. Unthankfulness is listed as one of the notable sins of the "last days" (II Tim. 3:1-2). It is the mother of almost every human vice.

I seriously disagreed with the pastor's message from II Corinthians 5:18. Candidly, I cannot give God thanks for everything, nor can I understand everything as being the will of my heavenly Father. How could any sane person give thanks to God for the lives and deeds of Adolf Hitler, Joseph Stalin, Karl Marx, V.I. Lenin, Charles Darwin, Nimrod, Ahab, Jezebel and the countless other infamous rogues of human history? Nor can I "thank and praise God" for murder, robbery, anarchy, adultery, sodomy, fornication, prostitution, lies, gambling, drunkenness, broken homes, starving children, butchered teenagers with their brains fried by drugs. As a foreign missionary, I have seen numerous demon-possessed persons: torn, violent, screaming, vomiting, smashing to the floor or against walls in powerful convulsions. For such things I cannot thank God. Satan must be credited for such debauchery.

Which informed, soul-winning Christian worker could get on his knees and thank God for the cults such as the Jehovah's Witnesses, the Mormons or the mystic, pagan Eastern religions? No born-again, informed Christian who means business with God could ever "praise the Lord" for the Mass of the Roman Catholic Church in which millions are deceived into believing they are actually eating the "literal flesh" of Jesus Christ and the priests actually drinking the "literal blood" of God's dear Son. All this despite the stern warnings of Leviticus 17:11-14 and total consensus of the first churches that consuming literal blood was forbidden (see Acts 15:6, 23, 28-29). This horrendous practice is based on an extreme literal interpretation of Jesus' great sermon in John 6:35-59. (See with this Hebrews 10:14 and I Peter 3:18, which state that Christ's death was "once for all" and not thousands of times daily on papal altars round the world.) I cannot thank God for such perversions of truth. Men are saved through repentance and faith in Christ, not by eating His flesh, and the priest drinking His blood. (See Chapter 19.)

As I look about society today, and over my past life, there must be thousands of things for which I cannot thank God, simply because I believe He had nothing to do with them. I understand the texts listed at the beginning of this chapter to say that we are to "thank God" for all things that come from God. We read that God inhabits the praises of His people (Psa. 22:3) and that "It is a good thing to give thanks unto the Lord" (Psa. 92:1). God desires that we give Him praise and thanks for everything for which He is responsible. We cannot praise God for the works of the Devil. Such actions would be an abomination. Proverbs 16:4 declares: "The Lord hath made all things for Himself: yea even the wicked for the day of evil." God has never made a man wicked, sinful and unholy, even though He does make (or bring into being) certain men for His own special purposes in this world (see Ex. 9:16 with Rom. 9:17-18 and Isa. 44:28; 45:1).

We read in Ecclesiastes 7:29 how God originally made man: "Lo, this only have I found, that God hath made man upright: but they have sought out many inventions." Man became a rebel and sinner by personal choice and deliberate action. God did not make him go this way. The text in Proverbs 16:4 states that God has made the wicked (man) for the (his) day of evil, and not that He has made the wicked man to be wicked. He became godless and corrupt by his own volition and selection. We are sure that the wicked person's day(s) of evil will include whatever judgments God may send upon his head in this life (see examples of this in Ahab, I Kings 22:37-38; Jezebel in II Kings 9:30-35; others in Psa. 12:1-3; 21:8-12; 58:3-7 and Acts 12:21-23). It will also include their day of evil in everlasting hell. In this sense "God has made the wicked for the day of evil." Similar comments are applicable to Isaiah 45:7, where the created evil has reference to God's voracious, terrible judgments.

This chapter is not intended to be a theological treatise on the mystic sovereignty or providence of the Almighty. Rather, it is a layman's book. I cannot thank God for Satan or sin and its universal ravages. Personally, I understand that Satan became so of his own free choice (see the "I wills" of Lucifer in Isa. 14:12-14), never by some deliberate act or work of God. All the diabolical tyrants and false religions previously mentioned came into being by the devious machinations of men with the assistance of Satan and demons. God made none of them. But He has made for all of them their day of evil. Bloody, godless, murderous communism came into being not because God created it, but by the demon-inspired connivance of beastly men and women who freely made themselves available to the Devil and sin. God had nothing to do with it. Mentally normal human beings do have a will, even a free will (see Ezra 7:13 for free will). Man can "choose" (Josh. 24:15; Prov. 1:29; 3:31; Isa. 56:4) and man has a will to "refuse"

73

(Neh. 9:16-17; Est. 1:12; Psa. 78:10; Prov. 1:24). What a man continually wills to do, that he will be.

Clearly, many things are of God, while others are not. It is certainly not so easy to always distinguish between the two. Looking back, I can sincerely thank God that He tackled me on that football field so many years ago. But it has taken decades for me to see this. Like the men on the Emmaus Road: "But their eyes were holden that they should not know him" (Lk 24:16), we also are often blind to the nearness of our Savior in life's greatest traumas. For God wills it so, frequently in the experience of His children.

After His resurrection from the dead, Jesus walked about the land for forty days and nights (Acts 1:3). During this period He appeared, "Not to all people, but unto witnesses chosen before God . . . " (Acts 10:41). It puzzled me for years why, in at least eleven different such appearings, our Lord took on (as it were) a disguise. Only a few times did His own disciples recognize Him, and even then it was mostly with a mixture of doubt and fear. Now I understand this mystery a little better. Is it not the same today? Our Lord comes to us in various disguises and we still fail to discern "It is the Lord" (John 21:7). Then our doubts and fears cloud the issue (Matt. 28:16,17). Nevertheless, the tender response of Christ is ever the same: "And He said unto them, Why are ye troubled? and why do thoughts arise in your hearts?" (Lk 24:38). As the terrified disciples "shut (the) doors" out of fear, we too, often miss His threefold benediction: "Peace be unto you" (John 20:19,21,26). We also shut the doors.

In our frequent blindness we simply fail to discover our Master in the sufferings that befall us over life's journey. For those Christians truly entrusted to the Savior every bitter spring of "Marah" will, in God's time, be made sweet (Ex. 15:23-25). Every "young lion that roars against us" will at a future date yield handfuls of delicious, fresh honey; enough even for others to share (Judges 14:5-6, 8-9). Is it not written that "Iron sharpeneth iron . . . " (Prov. 27:17)? Though the sorrows and pains sent into our lives as part of our calling and work for God often seem to destroy us, we have the sure word of proven experience from the heartbroken prophet, Hosea, whose adulterous wife nearly killed him: ". . . for he (God) hath torn, and he will heal us; he hath smitten, and he will bind us up" (Hos. 6:1). Is a fearful tornado crashing through your life? "Destroy it not; for a blessing is in it . . . " (Isa. 65:8). Our Lord rebuked the fierce wind and it obeyed Him (see Matt. 8:26)!

We refuse to thank God for sin and to credit Him with the works of the Devil. Joyfully, we should praise and thank our heavenly Father for what His "vocare" has planned for our lives. David understood this when he wrote: "My times are in thy hand . . . " (Psa. 31:15 and Psa. 37:23).

Though frequently very difficult to do, we are called upon to thank God "IN everything," but not "FOR everything" unless it is "unto Himself." Another part of our great and grand "vocare."

Chapter 14

―••⊕⊕⊕⊕••―

Stop Trying to Figure it All out

For over four years now my wife and I have struggled with the grim reality that our son was struck down with cancer of the bone marrow. Like millions of other Christians, we wondered "Why?". I am learning from Holy Scripture that it is not always sinful to ask God "Why?" concerning the storms of life. The Lord Jesus, hanging from Calvary's cross, questioned His Father in heaven with this pitiful cry: "My God, my God, why hast thou forsaken me?" (Psa. 22:1; 42:9; 74:1; 88:14). To question the Almighty from a heart of malice, with evil surmisings, would indeed be sinful. To sincerely question God from a pure conscience, void of offense and bitterness, does not cancel faith. Rather it proves it. I cannot list the times I have questioned God from a broken heart, distraught mind and out of a simple absence of understanding and purpose. In love and mercy He listened to and understood all of them! Over the last few years I am rediscovering Revelation 2:10: "Fear none of these things which thou shalt suffer. Be thou faithful unto death, and I will give thee a crown of life." When we can discover no purpose in our sorrows, then we fear them and they haunt us.

Concerning our sick and suffering son — frankly I felt I knew some people who were more fitting candidates for the disease than he. But God does not see into the present life nor the future as we do (Isa. 55:8-9). And with some of the sorrows of life, in time, a few rays of dawn now begin to shoot forth. Looking back over many of our trials and sufferings, some things are coming into clearer focus. Some of the reasons "Why?" are now becoming clear. But only a few! However, these few glow with meaning.

Because Timothy was in the cancer ward of the Johannesburg

Hospital, we were there day and night. Debbie was also there. A lovely young mother and housewife, she too had been struck by the terrible disease. Sitting in a wheelchair, she listened intently as I explained to her the way of salvation. Within five minutes she gladly bowed her head in humble prayer and received the Lord Jesus Christ as her personal Savior. The doctors assured her she would recover as her sickness was only "chronic" not "acute." Several weeks later Debbie was in eternity! Here was one startling reason "Why?". For Debbie to be saved!

Young Stephen Jackson was in the room adjoining our son during the early stages of his illness. I purposely visited Stephen and befriended him. Leaving the hospital late one Saturday night, I felt compelled to enter his room. He wanted to talk and put his life right with God. He did. The next morning Stephen died. Then there was the businessman sitting at our lunch table one Wednesday. Our son, who was at that time in "remission" was also present for the meal. About midway through, our visitor stopped, looked over at Timothy and said: "Tim, because you have suffered with cancer, I have been saved. Thank you!" I almost burst into tears of joy and praise to God, for I had led this man to Christ some two months previously. I cannot describe the expression of happiness that beamed from our son's face upon hearing those words. Paul told the Corinthians that his sufferings had fallen out to their salvation (II Cor. 1:6). It continues so to this very hour.

In quiet moments of meditation and thoughtfulness over our son's terrible experience and sickness, I can see that it's starting to make more sense now. I can also see purpose and God in many of the sufferings of my life even though I have failed the Savior so often. In this age of saving grace how deeply thankful we all should be that God no longer turns those who "look back" into pillars of salt (Gen. 19:26). However, salt or not, most of the earthquakes that crash and smash into our lives will never be understood in this world. For God makes it so. It is during these difficult times that we must trust, even times when we must discipline ourselves to believe — when we seemingly cannot believe!

It is written: "Then the Lord answered Job out of the whirlwind . . . " (Job 38:1). All of our whirlwinds, however, do not carry the voice of God with the "answers" we search for. Nevertheless, in love we must continue to hope in our Lord, even when nothing makes sense any more, for " . . . He worketh all things after the counsel of His own will" (Eph. 1:11). And part of that holy will is "Suffering and Death: The Saints' Highest Calling."

Perhaps at this moment you are broken from some trial or burden which you feel is no longer bearable. The heartache is crushing you almost beyond repair. Read the words of Simon Peter: "But let none of you suffer as a murderer, or as a thief, or as an evil doer, or as a busybody in other men's matters" (I Peter 4:16). That is, don't suffer for sin; make an inventory and assure yourself that there is no known unconfessed and unforsaken sin in your life (see Prov. 28:13). If not, then receive your sufferings and trials as from the hand of God, even part of your holy career and ministry. Peter, the ex-fisherman who some thirty years earlier had denied his Lord with cursings and frenzied oaths, advises his readers with these comforting words: "Yet if any man suffer as a Christian, let him not be ashamed; but let him glorify God on this behalf" (I Peter 4:16).

If the millions of suffering saints could see their trials, pains, sicknesses and sorrows as part and parcel of their duties from God, part of their calling, part of their particular ministries, then they could "glorify God on this behalf." David did when he said: "It is good for me that I have been afflicted . . . " (Psa. 119:71). Paul and Silas did, even at the dark midnight hour in the filthy prison at Philippi (Acts 16:25), offering up prayers and praise.

Stop trying to "figure it all out," for you cannot. If God should choose to lift the curtain and offer you just a glimpse of the reason for your trials and sufferings (which mostly He won't), then you are to love and trust Him all the more for this special blessing. There is another view to our sorrows: that the Eternal God, the Supreme, Sovereign King of kings and Lord of lords, would choose that we redeemed mortals could by our trials, sorrows, storms and griefs somehow reflect the likeness of Christ. And that we could demonstrate our oneness with Him, be as He was in the world (I John 4:17), partake of His sufferings by bearing "His cross" (Lk 14:27 with Matt. 10:38) is to be honored from heaven. Poor frustrated and bewildered Job, trying to put it all together, finally gave vent to what is becoming our prayer also: "Though he slay me, yet will I trust in him . . . " (Job 13:15). It is all part of our heavenly calling, our God-given "vocare." Though we mostly do not understand what God is doing with us and for us, we love Him still with a madness and passion, even when we see His loving hand poised to slay us. Only could this be grace operative in our hearts.

Near the conclusion of several years of unbroken trials, extraordinary suffering and unanswered prayers, Job refused any longer to look for the reasons "why?". He said: " . . . I will lay mine hand upon my mouth" (Job 40:4). Looking back, I regret not having done the same during many of the darkest hours of my Christian life. In the ancient culture of Job's day, the hand over the mouth was the sign that no more debate or argument was forthcoming. It signaled that the sufferer had stopped trying to figure it all out. He had surrendered to (but not understood) the events that had fallen upon his life.

So often, weaker Christians, fret in painful anxiety as they anticipate what next may befall them on tomorrow. If only our poor hearts could remember that God is, even today, already there in tomorrow and has all its troubles under His control.

Perhaps we work too hard trying to make sure we never become "fools for Christ's sake." And usually we are rather successful at this fitful and arduous task.

No mortal being knows the total truth about anything in this life, especially the mountainous sufferings of humanity. An ancient fable illustrates this: Once the sun fell into argument with the moon. The sun declared: "The leaves on earth are green." The moon retorted that leaves are mostly silver in color. The moon affirmed, men generally sleep on earth, but the sun shouted that men on earth are always rushing about.

Then the moon asked: "But why is there such silence down there?" "And who told you that?" replied the sun. "On earth there is always much noise." So the quarrel lasted for many months.

The wind came and listened to their debate. "You argue in vain" he said. "I blow over earth when both of you shine. I am present by day and night. During day when sun shines, everything happens on earth just as the sun has said. Leaves are green, earth is filled with noise and men hurry to and fro. I am also present at night. When moon rises to do his work, earth changes. Leaves turn silver, men mostly sleep and silence falls over nearly all things. Neither of you, sun, nor moon, know the total truth!"

We too, are as the sun and moon. Our best arguments are limited. God warns us ". . . we know in part" (I Cor. 13:9). The saint who determines to find the answers to all of life's trials and sorrows will end his career in the madhouse. Such a thing God will not allow. So be wise hurting Christian. Stop trying to figure it all out. Trust God if it kills you. It might too!

Chapter 15

Where Is the Joy of the Lord?

How can the joy of the Lord promised in Holy Scripture, ever be reconciled with the Christian's calling to suffer, to be subjected to trials and afflictions, and ultimately to experience physical death? Among thousands of believers there exists the disturbingly erroneous belief that, with personal salvation of the soul, there comes an iron-clad, money-back guarantee that promises the newly born-again Christian almost total immunity from all suffering. The saved suddenly become "exempt" from the sorrows, grief, losses, heartaches, afflictions, pains, sicknesses and disappointments of human life. From numerous pulpits, T.V. and radio programs we hear: "Come to Jesus; be saved and all your problems will be solved." Such fallacious preaching has produced as many casualties among conservative Christians as the wild extremes of the "faith healers" and the "wealthy-healthy" cults. In this respect one is as bad or dangerous as the other. The unconverted man who sincerely comes to Christ, not only trusting for his soul's salvation, but also for "all his problems to be solved," faces deep frustrations and bitter experiences in the months, and years, that follow. And why? For the reason God has made no such promise to His children in all the 31,175 verses of Holy Scripture.

A full month's instruction in Luke 14:25-35 would be one of the best ways to demolish some of the destructive illusions that accompany such untrue representations of God's gift of eternal life. We are saved to serve, as these verses demonstrate, and Christ relates these passages strictly to serving: Right priorities (verse 26), cross-carrying (verse 27), the cost of building (verses 28-30), fighting a war (verses 31-32) and forsaking things that are clearly sinful (verse 33). It is noteworthy that Paul concluded his first

83

missionary journey by sternly admonishing his converts: " . . . we must through much tribulation enter into the kingdom of God" (Acts 14:22). Over twenty years later, Paul ended his service for Christ by instructing his convert Timothy: ". . . be thou partaker of the afflictions of the gospel according to the power of God" (II Tim. 1:8). Gospel "afflictions" can only be borne "by the power of God," and all of them are simply the natural fruit of our "vocare" from the Lord.

A critical missing element in today's evangelism, church-planting, missionary work, new convert classes and Christian preaching-teaching in general is the overwhelming truth of Holy Scripture: we must suffer for Christ and be tried for our faith. A faith that is not tried, even in the fire, is worthless. It is not the faith of God's Word and true Christian history. Those who conceal these facts from their young converts, for fear that they will turn away from following the Savior are doing both their converts and the testimony of Jesus Christ a severe injustice. No doubt, the philosophy behind such reasoning is sincere, but sincerity does not save it from being dangerously false. Those who, even slightly, insinuate to young converts that heaven may now be entered "on flowery beds of ease" are guilty of serious misinformation that wounds and injures God's little children. Our calling from heaven to suffer should not be understood as a "self-inflicted" martyrdom. There is nothing fatalistic or ruinous about fulfilling heaven's will and "vocare" for the Christian's life.

When God called Paul into the ministry it was with a shocking announcement: "For I will shew him how great things he must suffer for my name's sake" (Acts 9:16). Note, not "bad things" or "horrible things," but "great things . . . for my name's sake." Can it be that God actually counts suffering in His name as a "great thing"? In the pages of this book the fact of Christian suffering has been established. God does consider it great.

But how is such suffering reconciled with the joy of God in our hearts? The second fruit of the indwelling Holy Spirit is "joy" (Gal. 5:22). Where does this fit in? A clear distinction must be made between the joy of Christ and that of circumstances, profit, the social and temporal benefits of everyday life. Atheists, sinners of the worst kind, rejectors of Christ and the unsaved in general have their experiences of joy. I remember seeing a film of Adolf Hitler "dance with joy" as his panzers invaded Poland. More recently, I saw an Australian farmer jumping and shouting because he had just won a $1,000,000.00 lottery. Proverbs 2:14 speaks of persons void of wisdom ". . . who rejoice to do evil. . . ." But the joy of the unsaved is a world apart from that of the saved Christian walking in fellowship with his Lord. A sense of appreciation and expressions of thankfulness are not necessarily the exclusive right of a true child of God. Unbelievers also experience such moments. But our sense of appreciation and thankfulness springs from a vastly different source. They are based on unique priorities and are an exclusive feature of the redeemed.

With a prisoner's chain on his left wrist, Paul wrote to fellow believers: "Rejoice in the Lord alway: and again I say, Rejoice" (Phil. 4:4). I have preached in jails dozens of times and never yet have I seen a single prisoner "rejoicing" as he sat behind steel bars. Clearly the joy of the saved is not that of the unsaved. The joy of knowing sins forgiven is not rooted in geographical locations or physical circumstances — rather it is in a Person. The eternal Son of God, even our Lord Jesus Christ.

The joy of a soul saved from sin springs from within (Gal. 4:6), even from our hearts. We ". . . joy in God" because of Christ's atonement (Rom. 5:11). The salvation of lost souls brought ". . . great joy" to the city of Samaria (Acts 8:8). Paul's converts were to him "joy," even a "crown of rejoicing" (I Thess. 2:19). David wrote: "We will rejoice in thy salvation" (Psa. 20:5). This is true joy. In Colossians 1:24, Paul said that he ". . . rejoiced in his sufferings," not in his fame as a missionary. He understood these sufferings to be God's "vocare" for his life and ministry. He found joy in them. Holy Scripture declares the cause of our joy is different from that of the lost world. "Blessed are ye when men shall revile you, and persecute you, and shall say all manner of evil against you falsely, for my sake. Rejoice and be exceeding glad: for great is your reward in heaven . . . " (Matt. 5:11-12). Only a heart transformed by a miracle from God could rejoice in such sufferings. Christ instructed his disciples in the tap-root reason for all true joy: ". . . because your names are written in heaven" (Lk 10:20). No unconverted soul has this priceless possession. Because of Christ's saving death our names are written in heaven. What a basis for offering praises to God!

When everything seems to indicate failure, when nothing makes sense any more, and when our sufferings and sorrows appear to smother the promises of our Lord's help, the Bible declares: ". . . (God) hath said, I will never leave thee, nor forsake thee" (Heb. 13:5). The responsibility lies squarely on Him to do this. And He will! Are you stumbling in some awful night? The Old Testament prophet did and he wrote: ". . . when I sit in darkness, the Lord shall be a light unto me" (Micah 7:8). Job said: ". . . He giveth songs in the night" (Job 35:10). Mysterious Habakkuk saw a burden from the Lord (Hab. 1:1). As God's watchman on the tower, he envisaged national destruction and summarized the calamity in the final passages of his marvelous little book. "Although the fig tree shall not blossom, neither shall fruit be in the vines; the labor of the olive shall fail, and the fields shall yield no meat; the flock shall be cut off from the fold, and there shall be no herd in the stalls: Yet will I rejoice in the Lord, I will joy in the God of my salvation" (Hab. 3:17,18). Few of us have been pushed into Habakkuk's corner. When every visible, tangible cause for earthly happiness and joy vanished, the prophet found satisfaction in his Lord. "Things" were swept away; God was there! Early Christian missionaries on the island of Madagascar, stripped of earthly possessions, even their clothes, marched off to their martyrdom, rejoicing and loudly singing hymns of praise and thanks to their Savior. Theirs' was the joy of the Lord. The world, with its passions and appeals, its promises and pleasures, offers no such hope.

We reject the nonsense of a "trouble-free salvation." The Jesus who will "solve all your earthly problems" is foreign to Holy Scripture. The Christian faith has never been a religious panacea. Nor do we swing to the opposite extreme of a "doom gloom" life,

86

bored stiff by the "thou shalt not's" of our faith. The joy of the Lord is our priceless treasure in earthen vessels (II Cor. 4:6-7). "Things" and "men" did not grant it, neither can they steal it. As with Habakkuk, God is our joy. Sadly, we may, in dark moments, fail to live in the comfort of this wonderful truth. I surely have.

Our Savior had "joy set before him." Ultimately, it was the joy of saving millions of lost souls who would repent and believe in His atonement. Before He could enter into this joy Jesus had to ". . . endure the cross" (Phil. 2:8). This cross entailed six hours of the greatest suffering ever experienced in human flesh and recorded in earth's history. The "vocare" of Christ was likewise one of suffering and pain. To grasp this joy ". . . he humbled himself, and became obedient unto death, even the death of the cross" (Phil. 2:8). Always there must be a cross before the joy and a night before the next glorious dawning.

Often while laboring under the load of afflictions and sharp trials, or a flesh racked by unspeakable pain, we catch a glimmer of God's hammer nailing us upon the cross of a fresh death. All of this prepares our hearts for the next step in our calling, being ever humbled and broken. Then suddenly our weary minds and distraught souls are warmed and loved by the sunrise of true joy. It is unspeakable! Now we understand better the ode of the Psalmist: ". . . weeping may endure for a night, but joy cometh in the morning" (Psa. 30:5). This too is our portion.

Do not cheapen the joy of the Lord. It is priceless, yet so costly. Amid a dangerous situation of civil strife, potential revolution, death threats and political turmoil, Nehemiah admonished his followers: ". . . for the joy of the Lord is your strength" (Neh. 8:10). Deeply contemplating the sovereignty of God's prophecies about the future crucifixion of His Son, David instructs the kings and judges of earth in the proper attitude of service and joy: "Serve the Lord with fear, and rejoice with trembling" (Psa. 2:11). Joy in the souls of the redeemed, tempered by a holy, trembling reverence, is the true joy of the Lord.

The curse of omnipresent Hollywood-style evangelism and a

cheapened, vulgar flesh-centered type of Gospel preaching has resulted in the joy of the Lord being blurred and exchanged for "strange fire" (Num. 3:4). Now we hear "Let's get happy" or "Come on, everybody, join in the fun." Alas! do not confuse the joy of our Lord with a trip to the circus, a ride on the merry-go-round, or a weekend on the beach with all expenses paid. Such bright but carnal thrills and fleshly stimulants fade as the flowers. God's joy and delights are not demonstrated in the uncouth, theatrical performances being given by many of today's "famed Holy Ghost-anointed" preachers and special singers. Their dress, hairstyles, body language, coarse jesting, nightclub presentation of Jesus, mixture of wrong with right; the flippant and frivolous remarks about sin, hell, Satan and God's terrible judgments do not reflect the demeanor of genuine Spirit-filled Christians. Possibly these jesting clowns and buffoons are best described in Psalm 59:6: "They return (appear) at evening: they make a noise like a dog, and go round about the city." The Egyptian philosophy, ". . . and the people sat down to eat and drink, and rose up to play" (Ex. 32:6), does not express the joy of the Lord. Its origin is in hell below.

True Christian joy is designed to cheer our broken spirits amid the darkest night. But often our load is so crushing that we miss the good comfort of such help. God has called us into a service that involves all these experiences because "His desire is towards (us)" (Song 7:10). Peter, writing to persecuted saints scattered over most of Asia, dared to say: ". . . ye rejoice with joy unspeakable and full of glory" (I Peter 1:1,8). Our heavenly "vocare" was properly described by the apostle Paul "As sorrowful, yet always rejoicing" (II Cor. 6:10).

Soon the winter and tempests of human life will be over and we may confidently anticipate what is shadowed in the beautiful Song of Songs: "For, lo, the winter is past, the rain is over and gone; The flowers appear on the earth; the time of singing of the birds is come, and the voice of the turtle is heard in our land; The fig tree putteth forth her green figs, and the vines with the tender grape give a good smell" (Song 2:11-13). In glowing, colorful terms the Hebrew hymnist seems to express a longing for the dawn of heaven's eternal joy. That is part of our hope, for it is the everlasting consummation of the saints' highest calling.

In the world of botany, some plants are heliotropic and others are asphodels. The latter grow only in deep shade or total darkness. Heaven's great botanist works carefully that His born-again asphodels may grow through their hardships, sorrows and long seasons of darkness. I have observed that men who suffer most love God the greatest. In the lives of such people we see the joy of the Lord in truth.

Chapter 16

Our Final Call

I have referred to physical death as a calling from God. Even our final call. It is a work He has assigned each of us to do, to perform, for His glory. In Ecclesiastes 3:1-2, we discover that death is spoken of as a "time" and a "purpose under heaven." In these passages it is also called "a season." Here Scripture informs us that death is also part of God's purpose for our lives. Each child of God is called of God to finally ". . . walk through the valley of the shadow of death" (Psa. 23:4). In Hebrews 9:27 we learn that death is an "appointment" all must keep. When King David faced death he said to his son Solomon: "I go the way of all the earth" (I Kings 2:2). We shall all go that way (unless our Lord returns beforehand). Every man must enter into his "season" of death (see Job 7:1).

Some tell us from both pulpit and printed page that God has nothing to do with death. It is looked upon as coming from the Devil himself. Somehow, it almost represents a grand victory over God, for Satan and evil. These views are seriously ill-informed. Physical death is the final ministry in which all of God's children will share; none will be exempt. Though in this life our careers and vocations may vastly differ, every one of us is called from heaven to die. It's our final duty for Christ and should be performed with the highest integrity and honor. The crowning point of Christian service — our last witness.

As joy in the life of a saved Christian cannot be the same as joy in the life of the unconverted, so it is with death. For the child of God death is a defeated foe. When death claimed the life of the Son of God on the cross, it made the biggest mistake! Old man death stood like a conquering tyrant over the expired body of Christ for three days and nights. But no longer! The worldwide authority and rule of death collapsed when God, by the Holy Spirit, in resurrection power, gave old man death the knockout blow. We read of the lifeless body of Jesus: "Whom God hath raised up, having loosed the pains of death: because it was not possible that He should be holden of it" (Acts 2:24). We learn from Romans 8:11 and I Peter 3:18 that God delivered His Son from the hold of death by the power of the Holy Spirit. This was death's defeat.

During the earthly ministry of Christ, Scripture speaks of three people He raised from death: a little girl in Mark 5:35-43; a young man in Luke 7:11-17 and a grown man in John 11. There can be no doubt that Christ raised hundreds of which Scripture says nothing. These three examples clearly demonstrate that Christ defeated death in all three stages of human life (childhood, teenage and adulthood). Every person the Lord Jesus raised had to die again and their bodies remain dead to this moment. But the resurrection of Christ is for ever! "Knowing that Christ being raised from the dead dieth no more; death hath no more dominion over him" (Rom. 6:9). The terrifying hornet of death had its needle permanently extracted when it stung the Holy One from heaven. Now He lives for ever! Realizing this comforting truth, Paul defies physical death and the grave with these words: "O death, where is thy sting? O grave, where is thy victory?" (I Cor. 15:55). The Lord Jesus dramatically and eternally conquered death for Himself and for all who trust Him as their personal Savior. In His defeat of death and bodily resurrection (breaking free from death's prison, the grave) Christ for ever demonstrated that He is, in fact, the Son of God: "And (Jesus was) declared to be the Son of God with power, . . . by the resurrection from the dead" (Rom. 1:4). Paul wrote to Timothy of the Savior: ". . . who hath abolished death, and hath brought life and immortality to light through the Gospel" (II Tim. 1:10). In Revelation 1:18 Christ announced Himself as follows to fearful John: "I am He that liveth, and was dead; and, behold, I am alive for evermore, Amen; and have the keys of hell and death." Christ's victory over physical death, assures believers that our dreaded enemy is now a dear friend. (Death for the unsaved, however, is their doorway into hell. And the hell of Scripture is not the grave, unconsciousness or annihilation as the cults teach. See Matt. 13:47-51; II Thes. 1:7-9 and Rev. 14:11.)

When our God vanquished death, broke its steel grip from His Son's dead body, stripped death of its power, ripped the keys from its belt, He changed death for the born-again believer. Death is no longer for the saved child of God "the king of terrors" (Job 18:14). Jesus Christ has "delivered us from the fear of death" and its steel "bondage" (Heb. 2:15). But rarely is this understood. Death is now God's messenger, sent to fetch His children home! In Revelation 6:8 the "pale horse and his rider, death," receive their orders from God alone. No wonder it says in Psalm 116:15: "Precious in the sight of the Lord is the death of his saints." Death is the doorway into heaven and once Christians get a firm grip of this glorious truth they too are ". . . willing rather to be absent from the body and present with the Lord" (II Cor. 5:8). Our blessed Lord, having conquered death, will some day call us to go via that doorway. It is our final work for Him. Death is now our free ticket to the "place" Jesus went to prepare (John 14:2). It will chaperon us home. However, with the unsaved it will be a ghastly different story! This is fearfully illustrated in the words of the famed atheist and blasphemer, Sir Francis Newport. With inexpressible horror he screamed from his deathbed: "Oh, the insufferable pangs of hell!" and died. Alas, the shocking destiny of those who die unsaved! (See Chapter 19.)

Christ's resurrection converted death into the saint's friend. This resurrection power transforms monsters into gentle men, witches into kind women, beer into milk, wine into wages, lust into love, hate into harmony, and sinners into saints. This is the same power that will sustain all true believers in their "vocare" of suffering and finally dying.

It is wonderfully true that, in this life, God heals and saves from physical death when it is His will (I John 5:14-15). As stated earlier, such amazing miracles are not always His will for the lives of His children. Charlatans and the untaught have seized upon the

93

various passages that speak of healing and twisted these into a "come-one-come-all, worldwide, no-one-exempt, it's for everybody" theology. The philosophy that states: "Because the Bible records that Jesus, Paul, Peter or whoever in Scripture performed earth-shaking miracles, it is our guarantee that we can do the same," is misleading and destructive. It is a gross misrepresentation of rightly divided Bible doctrine; it makes a false appeal to the weakness of the flesh and reveals an abysmal lack of insight into God's purpose for man and this age of grace. It fails to realize that suffering and death are companions of the saints.

Norva Spitzer lived in Greenville, South Carolina. He was a brilliant electrical engineer who spent his Christian life serving both God and man in humble quietness. Suffering from unspeakable pain due to arthritis, Norva went in for a physical checkup. To his shock, he was diagnosed as also having lung cancer. It was classified as being terminal. Family, friends and his entire church were shaken at the news. A special prayer meeting was called for the church and friends to pray for his healing. Upon returning home on furlough in 1992, we enjoyed an evening meal with this good man, his wife, our son Phillip and daughter-in-law, Sandra. Not many months later we attended Norva's funeral. God did not heal this Christian gentleman. Rather, he was needed in heaven. Never believe the ludicrous and loony nonsense that it is God's will to always heal every Christian of every sickness, every time, even if they do "meet all the conditions." If this were so, Christians could never die. Earth would become an everlasting old age home and heaven would soon be devoid of its final population.

Some believers are genuinely healed by the power of God; most are not. That is the bare truth of the matter. There may be numerous reasons for this, but it remains a fact just the same. Among saved, God-fearing Christians who have surrendered their bodies and lives to the Lord Jesus Christ, we do infrequently find those who have been miraculously healed. In some instances the best medical practitioners have been confounded. But such cases are exceptions, not rules. We must never forget that every authentic healing that saves from death was the choice of God Almighty to perform such a work. And, in every case not healed and the person died, it was the same God who made the decision not to heal. Both are from the same loving, heavenly Father. He sees best and acts ". . . according to the good pleasure of His will" (Eph. 1:5). But even those so marvelously healed eventually get sick again and will finally die. Death is our final call. Someone remarked: "You can't get out of this world alive."

In 1965, we were engaged in pioneer missionary work in the desert of central Australia. Our baby son, Phillip, about two years old, fell dangerously ill with pneumonia. In the grip of a freezing winter's night, he lay choking to death in his mother's arms. My wife and I were in the kitchen. She was seated in a chair embracing baby Phillip. Slipping to the cold floor on my knees, I cried out to God this prayer: "Lord, if you are pleased to let us have our son, then I ask you to heal him. If not, we give him to you." Instantly, God healed the struggling, choking child. He sprang up in his mother's arms, laughing, ready to play! We both were stunned at such an immediate demonstration of great power, being filled with the fear of God at this sudden miracle of healing. Later on the same child, as a grown man, contracted a curious illness of which he has never been healed. He suffers from it even today. This is how God works. Strange but wonderful! "O the depth of the riches both of the wisdom and knowledge of God! how unsearchable are his judgments, and his ways are past finding out" (Rom. 11:33). With Paul we whisper: "But who hath known the mind of the Lord, that he may instruct him?" (I Cor. 2:16). This healing of our baby son was a genuine miracle from the hand of God. Not the cheap, vulgar, side-show demonstration seen in the extreme charismatic circus.

Divine healings are, at the greatest, only temporary. As time marches on, death draws closer and closer. Then it summons us away. The vocation to die is especially sacred and hallowed, because it is the final call God will send to His blood-bought children. Paul, knowing the date was set for his execution by the Roman sword, triumphantly says to Timothy: "For I am now ready to be offered, and the time of my departure (to heaven and home) is at hand" (II Tim. 4:6). He was ready and eager to fulfil his final duty for God. Stephen, reflecting the likeness of his Savior, faced his last work for Christ in true Christian victory: "And he kneeled down, and cried with a loud voice, Lord lay not this sin to their charge." In verse 59 he prayed: "Lord Jesus, receive my spirit" (Acts 7:58-59). Peter, as an old man, penned these optimistic words to those of like precious faith: "Knowing that shortly I must put off this my tabernacle, even as our Lord Jesus Christ hath showed me" (II Peter 1:14 with John 21:17-19). He knew that the final call of God was just "shortly" away. Peter was ready to perform this heavenly duty with honor, by putting off his physical body.

In describing physical death as our final service to God, I am not attempting to present a "superman" theology. It is only normal to battle to the last breath, to keep our loved ones here with us. My eldest son, David, gave his brother a bone marrow transplant. This prevented Timothy from "dying before his time" (Eccl. 7:17). Because of this, we have enjoyed Tim's presence another three years. Our hearts ache, our tears flow, our minds become clouded amid the sufferings of ourselves, precious loved ones, and dearest friends and we fight hard to keep them alive. But ultimately death will beckon them and us away from this veil of tears. We must do all within our power to assist those who suffer and the terminally ill to die with assurance, Godly dignity and especially with a sense that this is God's last work for us to do. I want to fulfil this task to His honor and glory. Countless times in prayer I have asked God to let my death be my greatest sermon. Yes, even understanding this, so frequently I have considered my faith like the "tottering fence" of Psalm 62:3. But in this hope we do not totter: "I shall be satisfied, when I awake with (God's) likeness" (Psa. 17:15). Then, it will have been worth it all.

God's ownership of our souls and presence with us is profoundly reflected in this all covering promise: ". . . whether we live therefore, or die, we are the Lord's" (Rom. 14:9). We are His in this life as well as that which is to come.

Chapter 17

No Hope after Death: Dying to See Heaven

The comforting promises made for those who are God's children and called to the final "vocare" of facing death, sadly cannot be applied to the unsaved. Those without Christ as personal Lord and Savior are described in the Holy Bible as ". . . having no hope, and with-out God in the world" (Eph. 2:12). They are ". . . dead (to God and spiritual realities) in trespasses and sins" (Eph. 2:1). Indeed, the unsaved are said to be ". . . blind" (to sin's consequences) and under "the power (control) of Satan" (Acts 26:18). For men to die with sins unforgiven by God, to die without a saving knowledge of the Lord Jesus Christ, is to die a child of the Devil (I John 3:10). Contrary to popular opinion, the unsaved at death enter hell (see Psa. 9:17; 55:15; Matt. 10:28; Lk 16:19-31). This is not a parable as the cults teach (also see II Thess. 1:7). As surely as heaven is a place prepared by God for the redeemed, just as sure is hell a place prepared for the punishment of sin and sinners (Matt. 25:41). Let no reader of these lines be so gullible as to believe the Devil's popular lie that "Hell is only the grave." Death to the unconverted is life's most horrible experience. It is an eternal, fearful leap into everlasting darkness (Jude 13), the well-earned fate of special fools (Psa. 53:1), the horrible highway leading to the city of the damned (Matt. 7:13). As physical death calls the saved to heaven, so it will subpoena the unsaved to appear in the flames of a conscious, Christless eternity, one of never-ending damnation. Hence the warning: "Flee from the wrath to come" (Matt. 3:7). How to be saved from sin and the fate of hell is clearly explained in the final pages of this book. (See Chapter 19.)

However, this last service of physical death we are called

upon to perform for our heavenly Father will, for many, be the most difficult of all. For thousands it will involve days, weeks, months and even years of prolonged illness. It is written of Isaac: "And it came to pass, that when Isaac was old that he could not see . . . " (Gen. 27:1). (It is interesting that no one prayed for his healing!) I have known several who lingered for years in literal blindness, waiting for death to call them home. My heart filled with pity for these. Some of us will be required to bear a stroke, chronic heart attack, deafness or a fierce terminal disease. Over five million Americans sit in old-age homes waiting for death. Many of you who read these lines will be among that number in a few years' time. Now, while our minds are clear and functional, while we have a measure of health and strength, is the time to pray and plan towards our final "vocare," soon to come at the bidding of our loving heavenly Father.

The "terrors and sorrows of death" (Psa. 55:4 and Psa. 116:3) must be dealt with now, not when we are old, feeble and our minds are senile. Every Christian needs the presence and assistance of God as never before during the sunset of earth's short day. The "Song of the sons of Korah" concludes on the right note: "For this God is our God for ever and ever: He will be our guide even unto death" (Psa. 48:14). And as surely as God has called us into this final act of human life, He has promised to see us through it all. Whoever wrote Psalm 71 was contemplating old age and death; but he did so with fear and wondering. Listen to the deep pathos of his trembling pleas: "Cast me not off in the time of old age; forsake me not when my strength faileth" (verse 9). He continues: "Now also when I am old and grayheaded, O God, forsake me not" (verse 18). God responded to these pitiful prayers later through the prophet Isaiah: "And even to your old age I am he; and even to hoar (gray) hairs will I carry you . . . " (Isa. 46:4). Rest assured that God will "carry" us through whatever the valley of death may hold. Again, remember it is written: "When thou passest through the waters, I will be with thee . . . " (Isa. 43:2).

For some, death will fall ". . . swifter than a weaver's shuttle" (Job 7:6), or as God whispered to Ezekiel concerning his darling wife: "Son of man, I take away from thee the desire of thine eyes with a stroke" (Eze. 24:16). For other Christians it will take years to expire. But at life's end is the bright hope for which we have borne the heavy calumnies of this world and tried to serve our Savior. There waits our friend, death! God's messenger boy has been summoned to escort us home. With holy angels as navigators (Psa. 91:11 with Lk 16:22) we shall enter the triumphal train of the millions who have passed before, to be ushered into the presence of eternal deity. Then we shall enjoy God for ever!

At last, with redeemed vision our ". . . eyes shall see the King in his beauty" (Isa. 33:17). "We shall be like him . . . " (I John 3:2) and ". . . shall see his face" (Rev. 22:4). Perfect ears will rejoice at holy sounds: "And I heard as it were the voice of a great multitude . . . saying, Alleluia: for the Lord God omnipotent reigneth" (Rev. 19:6). Ah, home sweet home — Heaven! ". . . and the name of that city from that day shall be, The Lord is there" (Eze. 48:35). Our burning hunger for God, "As the hart panteth after the water brooks . . . " (Psa. 42:1), will be ended; for ". . . God himself shall be with them, and be their God" (Rev. 21:3). Our friend, death, will deliver us into "the land that is fairer than day," where ". . . God shall wipe away all tears from their eyes; and there shall be no more death, neither sorrow, nor crying neither shall there be any more pain: for the former things have passed away" (Rev. 21:4). That land shall be called, "Beulah: for the Lord delighteth in thee . . . " (Isa. 62:4).

To die physically is our final work and deed for God; our final ministry, sermon and song; our last witness for Christ. It must be only the best! The promise is ours: "And they shall be mine, saith the Lord of hosts, in that day when I make up my jewels . . . " (Mal. 3:17). Then, our long, joyful, but often difficult journey through Psalm 23 will have ended: ". . . in the house of the Lord for ever" (verse 6). Until then we are just dying to see heaven. With this, our final "vocare" will be completed. We will have "put off" our battle harness for ever (I Kings 20:11).

Chapter 18

Setting Your House in Order

When good King Hezekiah fell ill unto death, God delivered to him a special message by the mouth of His preacher Isaiah: "Thus saith the Lord, Set thine house in order: for thou shalt die and not live" (Isa. 38:1). Note: here it is God who instructs the king to "set his house in order" for death was near. "Setting the house in order" was a common Jewish expression. It had nothing to do with spiritual preparation before death comes: rather, this command dealt solely with the practical side of physical death. Christians boast of being "ready to meet the Lord." Usually this has reference only to the state of their souls and assurance that sins are forgiven; hence, a readiness to meet their Maker.

After four decades of total involvement in the work of God, serving as pastor, missionary, lecturer, Bible school principal and so forth, I can state there is another side of death that most Christians are not ready for. They have not set their houses in order. In some respects it appears to me that the dumb beasts of earth exercise deeper wisdom and greater foresight than man! Jeremiah declared: "Yea, the stork in the heaven knoweth his appointed times; and the turtle and the crane and the swallow observe the time of their coming" (Jer. 8:7). Isaiah agreed: "The ox knoweth his owner, and the ass his master's crib: but Israel doth not know, my people doth not consider" (Isa. 1:3). I have seen certain animals actually go and prepare to die. Few Christians practice such foresight. So many of God's people simply do not consider the need to make practical arrangements for their final ministry of death. In the following pages I have outlined for responsible readers some practical suggestions on the fine art of "setting your house in order" before death.

1. INSURANCE OR BURIAL FUND:

Frequently we meet those atomic Christians who sincerely believe that insurance is a dreadful sin. "It demonstrates a lack of faith in God," so we hear. Bluntly, I do not have this kind of faith and am thankful I don't. To me this is mere foolishness or even blind folly, not faith.

My regret now at the sunset of life, is that I do not have more insurance. It is expensive to die in today's world. Mortician, funeral and burial expenses will not drop. Surely wisdom dictates that we have something laid aside in the form of insurance or a burial fund to cover these necessities. Our loved ones left behind must not have this added burden imposed upon them through our lack of prudence or plain incompetence. Too little planning reveals slothfulness. Too much planning suggests a lack of trust in the living God. Believers must be balanced.

Christian responsibility requires that we provide for these things now. Wise King Jehoshaphat had his burial site prepared well in advance (see II Chron. 16:14). Joseph of Arimathaea loaned his tomb to the Lord Jesus, Who returned it three days and nights later (Matt. 27:57-60). Judah's best king, Josiah, was buried in his family cemetery, previously prepared (see II Chron. 35:24). The passage in Isaiah 22:16, speaks of men constructing their burial tombs in the rocks. (On preparing a burial site, see Genesis 50:5.)

Your body must be buried somewhere. Have you chosen a site? Make this decision now, as far as possible. Who will pay your funeral expenses? Do not load these duties on those who remain after your decease. Set your house in order — now. Insurance brokers are available to advise you, and the older insurance companies are normally the most trustworthy and reliable. Or start your own private burial fund account. (On preparation and planning for future events see Prov. 6:6-8; 22:3; 24:30-34 and Philemon 22).

2. HAVE A WILL MADE:

If you own anything of reasonable value, it is imperative that you have a valid, updated will. The basic purpose of any will is

twofold: (1) To keep the State from taking what you h.
(2) To prevent family members from fighting over w
This has been in vogue since the days of Christ (see I.
where two brothers approached Jesus about a disputed \
can prayerfully select to divide your earthly goods amon   _..ι
you may. Remember your Last Will and Testament is the correct
place to designate a portion of your money for the work of God.
Any legal firm or trusted individual lawyer can advise you
regarding the preparation of your will. This should be done
immediately. The financial cost for this service far outweighs the
problems that must arise if you die without leaving a signed will.
Thousands of Christians end life without such preparation. It is
sheer carelessness on their part and reflects a lack of consideration
for being "good stewards" of the things God has entrusted into their
keeping. "Not slothful in business" (Rom. 12:11) is the command
of God. (On the subject of leaving an inheritance or will, see Gen.
31:14; Num. 26:53; Jos. 1:6; Prov. 13:22; 17:2; 19:14; 20:21; Eccl.
7:11 and II Cor. 12:14).

3. LEAVE COMPLETE FUNERAL AND BURIAL INSTRUCTIONS:

A. Cremation is forbidden for Christians as it is a totally pagan-heathen custom having its origin in worship of demons. In I Corinthians 10:20, we are forbidden to have any "fellowship with demons." Cremation is further a major attempt of Satan to refute and confuse the physical resurrection of all men unto final judgment. In cases of loved ones dying with contagious/fatal diseases (e.g. AIDS), some believers feel it is justified to bypass the standard burial and resort to cremation. I have no opinion on this issue. "Let every man be fully persuaded in his own mind" (Rom. 14:5).

B. Where do you want your funeral conducted? It is our duty to decide this now (as far as possible). Why not the house of God, where God's Word has been faithfully proclaimed and His saints meet to worship and fellowship? Can you think of a better place for a Christian's funeral service to be conducted? (See Psa. 26;8; 42:4; 84:10; 122:1; Matt. 18:20

103

and Heb. 10:25).

C. Who will preach your funeral? No born-again child of God who has lived his life for Christ wants a "modernist infidel" or Bible-denying, unbelieving clergyman conducting his funeral. In such circumstances I would prefer not to have one at all! Choose a Bible-living-preaching man of God to give the final word. Keep the Devil's preachers at bay. Write it down in your funeral arrangements. Name the minister you wish to speak at your last service and list a substitute should he not be available. (See Psa. 149:6; Eze. 3:17; Rom. 1:16; Gal. 1:10; I Thess. 2:4 and Titus 2:1).

D. What do you want said at your funeral? Remember, this will be the last time you can witness to your friends, family, loved ones, workmates, etc. You can speak to them through the officiating minister. Put down on paper what you want preached. I have it stated in my funeral instructions that "he shall preach the message of salvation with all his strength." Have it made clear whom you wish to read your obituary and any other special items for public announcement. Don't ask a waffling pip squeak to speak on behalf of yourself or your Lord. (See Isa. 58:1; Jer. 22:29; Acts 8:35; 11:14; 20:21; I Cor. 2:2; Gal. 1:8 and II Tim. 4:2-3).

E. What hymns or solos do you wish to be sung? Select these now. Hymns that have warmed your heart and refreshed your soul over life's journey. My funeral hymnology shall be (1) The Old Rugged Cross, (2) All Hail the Power of Jesus' Name, and (3) When I Survey the Wondrous Cross. These are the monarchs of the Christian faith. (See Psa. 59:16; 95:1; 150:6; Eph. 5:19 and Rev. 5:9).

F. Burial clothes. Why not something you presently enjoy wearing or something similar? I have requested to be buried in my black suit, with white shirt and mild red tie. This will cut costs by several hundred dollars. Funeral shrouds are very expensive, and come without backs or pockets! (See Isa. 61:10).

G. Pall-bearers. Appoint these with a substantial number of alternatives. Immediate family members, loved ones, friends or fellow Christians can serve this function. (See Matt. 14:12 and Acts 8:2).

H. Where to be buried has been touched on under Item 1. Your burial plot should be chosen and paid for long before your decease, if possible. Cemeteries or Memorial Gardens with "perpetual care" service are preferable. Ensure that they allow small plaques to be attached to gravestones. (See Gen. 23:3-4, 20; Prov. 22:28 and John 11:34).

I. Bulletins with salvation tracts inserted should be given to every person attending your funeral service. In the atmosphere of death the biggest sinners present will not refuse this handout. Some courteous person assigned to this task can stand at the door and offer these to everyone present, but only as they leave. (See Psa. 68;11; Eccl. 11:1,6; Lk 24:47-48; Acts 16:32; Rom. 1:16; I Cor. 4:15; Heb. 4:12 and I Peter 1:23).

J. Public invitation should be given for the unsaved present. Remember this will be your final opportunity to win the lost to Christ. Request the officiating minister, who will preach the saving message of your Lord, to conclude your funeral service by inviting the unsaved to receive Jesus Christ as personal Lord and Savior. I have seen dozens of people saved kneeling by the casket of a deceased friend or loved one.

Men's hearts are stirred, broken, soft and open to God on such occasions. It would be criminal not to invite your friends to heaven at your farewell service. (See Matt. 11:28; John 7:37; I Cor. 9:22; II Cor. 5:20 and Rev. 22:17.)

K. Arrange to have the entire service tape recorded or video-taped. It would be a priceless treasure for family posterity. (See Prov. 10:7; Acts 9:39 and Rev. 14:13.)

L. Grave markers. Perhaps no point is as important as this. Years ago, as a boy strolling through an old family cemetery, I still remember the faded Gospel invitation chiseled in dark

105

gravestones. It went deep into my young heart. Prearrange to have an attractive plaque made to be attached to your gravestone. It can carry a short testimony of your salvation, to-the-point verses from the Bible, and a courteously worded appeal for the readers to receive Christ as their Lord and Savior. Years after your death you can still be speaking for your Savior through this simple little Gospel witness. (See Josh. 8:32 with 24:26; Isa. 32:20 and I Cor. 9:22.)

Here is a sample of a beautiful tombstone sermon.

All visitors:

> Here from eternity, I quoth to say;
> You also follow in my way.
> Prepare to meet God, young and old;
> The king of fools will lose his soul.
> Salvation, Christ has free to all;
> His precious blood cleanseth all who call.

"For whosoever shall call upon the name of the Lord shall be saved" Romans 10:13

(Name of the deceased)

Never forget that your funeral will be your final sermon to the saints and sinners in your circle of human life. Diligently pray, think and plan to make this your greatest witness for your wonderful Lord. Like Abel of the Old Testament, it was written of him thousands of years after he was murdered by his jealous, Devil-inspired brother: ". . . he being dead yet speaketh" (I John 3:12 with Heb. 11:4). Years after our departure from this life we can still "speak" for our Savior, the Lord Jesus Christ, through the methods and suggestions listed above.

Have all documents pertaining to your death, funeral and instructions for procedures properly attested, signed and sealed by a notary or official commissioner of oaths. Make several photocopies and personally (if possible) distribute these among trusted members of your family. Store all originals in a safe-deposit

106

box or bank vault. Your lawyer and minister should also have copies.

How wonderful it would be at the end of life's journey, and after the smoke from judgment has cleared, to hear our blessed Lord say these sweet words of approval:

"WELL DONE THOU GOOD AND FAITHFUL SERVANT ... " (Matt. 25:21).

May God give to each of us grace to fulfil and complete our highest calling: suffering and death through life's short day. When our "vocare" is finished and our work is over we shall join in that heavenly anthem with the redeemed of all ages, "Saying with a loud voice, Worthy is the Lamb that was slain to receive power, and riches, and wisdom, and strength, and honor, and glory, and blessing" (Rev. 5:12). And with those four and twenty elders we shall fall at His feet ". . . and worship Him that liveth for ever and ever" (Rev. 5:14).

A FINAL WORD FROM OUR FATHER IN HEAVEN

"O that they were wise, that they understood this, that they would consider their latter end!" (Deut. 32:29)

"Thus saith the Lord, Set thine house in order: for thou shalt die and not live" (Isa. 38:1)

Chapter 19

God's Plan for Your Salvation

In the pages of Holy Scripture God has clearly laid down the plan of salvation for all who will receive and believe it. This plan is revealed to us in the Person and work of the Lord Jesus Christ. The outline below is one of the simplest for directing the unsaved person to eternal life and forgiveness of all sins. There are six steps. If you are lost in sin without God, obey this plan and be saved.

STEP ONE: REALIZE THAT YOU ARE LOST IN SIN WHICH BRINGS ETERNAL DEATH

A. "For all have sinned, and come short of the glory of God" declares Romans 3:23. "All" means every human being of mentally responsible age.

B. "For there is no man that sinneth not" states I Kings 8:46. None are exempt. "Jews and Gentiles . . . they are all under sin" Romans 3:9. This means every nation as well as every person.

C. "If we say we have no sin, we deceive ourselves and the truth is not in us" says I John 1:8. Only Jesus was without sin. Only fools say they have not sinned.

D. "For there is not a just man upon the earth, that doeth good, and sinneth not" Eccl. 7:20. Even good and just people have sinned. All are sinners!

SUMMARY OF THE ABOVE:

These verses from the Holy Bible state emphatically that all men have sinned. Even moral, upright people are under sin's condemnation as well as the godless and wicked. There are no exceptions to this rule. Every human being of mentally responsible age falls under the curse of sin.

STEP TWO: THE BIBLE SAYS THAT GOD WILL JUDGE AND PUNISH ALL SIN

A. "And I will punish the world for their evil, and the wicked for their iniquity . . . " Isaiah 13:11. It is God Who says this to mankind. He's not joking!

B. "The fathers shall not be put to death for the children, neither shall the children be put to death for the fathers: every man shall be put to death for his own sin" Deuteronomy 24:16. Again it is God Who speaks. Each person is responsible for himself and will answer for his own sins.

C. "For the wages of sin is death . . . " Romans 6:23. This is eternal death in hell and the lake of fire.

D. ". . . and sin, when it is finished, bringeth forth death" James 1:15. This "death" is not annihilation nor is it soul-sleep in the grave. It is eternal conscious suffering.

SUMMARY OF THE ABOVE:

All men of all places and races have sinned and are sinners. God has said over and over in the Bible that He will judge and punish men for their sins. This punishment is everlasting conscious "death" in hell and the lake of fire for ever (see II Thess. 1:7-9 and Rev. 20:15). Do you realize that you are lost in sin and without God? If so, please read carefully the next section.

STEP THREE: RECOGNIZE THAT CHRIST DIED FOR YOUR SINS SO YOU DON'T HAVE TO DIE FOR THEM.

A. ". . . Christ died for our sins" I Corinthians 15:3. "Our" means you!

B. "But God commendeth his love toward us, in that while we were yet sinners, Christ died for us" Romans 5:8. "Us" means you and yours!

C. "(Jesus) who gave himself for our sins . . . " Galatians 1:4. You again!

D.   "For Christ also hath once suffered for (our) sins, the just (Himself) for the unjust (us), that He might bring us to God . . . " I Peter 3:18. Christ can bring you to God!

SUMMARY OF THE ABOVE

God took our sins and placed them on His willing Son, the Lord Jesus. Then God judged and punished Christ for our sins (that we should have been judged and punished for). Thus, we can escape God's fearful judgment on our sins by accepting the substitute, Who died in our place; Jesus Christ. This is the greatest demonstration of God's love, when He gave His Son to die in our place. (See John 3:16 and I John 4:9-11). God has judged and punished your sins in Christ on the cross. (See also Isa. 53:6 and I Peter 2:24). Do you understand that Christ has died for your sins in your place?

STEP FOUR: REMEMBER THAT YOUR GOOD WORKS OR DEEDS CANNOT SAVE YOUR SOUL.

A.   "Not by works of righteousness which we have done, but according to His mercy He saved us . . . " says Paul in Titus 3:5.

B.   "Who hath saved us, and called us with an holy calling, not according to our works" Paul's testimony of his salvation in II Timothy 1:9.

C.   "But we are all as an unclean thing, and all our righteousnesses are as filthy rags . . ." Isaiah's confession about man's own righteousness and good works in Isaiah 64:6.

D.   "Therefore by the deeds of the law there shall no flesh (human) be justified (saved) in His (God's) sight . . . " Romans 3:20.

SUMMARY OF THE ABOVE

Man can do no righteous deeds or perform any good works that will merit or bring salvation and forgiveness of sins. All our works for salvation are "filthy rags." By keeping the Jewish law, we cannot be justified in God's sight. (Note: Good deeds and righteous works are to be daily in our faith and lives after we have been saved. See Matt. 5:16; Gal. 3:10; Titus 3:8 and James 2:14-26.) Accept the fact

111

that you can do nothing to save yourself. You must rely on the love and mercy of God!

STEP FIVE: RESPOND BY TURNING FROM YOUR SINS AND COMING TO CHRIST

A. Paul said: ". . . but now (God) commandeth all men everywhere to repent" Acts 17:30. Repent means to turn away from your sins and turn to Jesus Christ.

B. Jesus said: ". . . except ye repent ye shall all likewise perish" Luke 13:3. God requires you to be totally sick of your sins and eager to give them up.

C. Jesus said: "Come unto me, all ye that labor and are heavy laden, and I will give you rest" Matthew 11:28. Are you tired of a life in sin without God? If so you are ready to be saved!

D. Again Jesus said: ". . . him (meaning you) that cometh to me I will in no wise cast out" (or refuse) John 6:37. Christ has promised not to turn YOU away. Remember He came into this world to save you!

SUMMARY OF THE ABOVE

Jesus Christ has invited lost sinners to come to Him. He has promised not to turn them away; but they must come to Him after repenting, or turning away from their sins and yearning sincerely to be saved and forgiven. He is waiting for you now.

STEP SIX: BELIEVE AND RECEIVE CHRIST AS YOUR LORD AND SAVIOR

A. "Believe on (trust Him to save and forgive you) the Lord Jesus Christ and thou shalt be saved." This was Paul's answer to a man asking how to be converted in Acts 16:30-31.

B. "But as many as receive Him (Christ), to them gave He power to become the sons (children) of God" John 1:12. A person receives Jesus Christ, the instant he fully trusts Him.

C. ". . . if thou shalt confess with thy mouth the Lord Jesus, and shalt believe in thine heart that God hath raised Him from the dead, thou shalt be saved" Romans 10:9. Say "YES" and

112

confess to the fact that Jesus died on the cross for your sins and rose from the dead to give you life. (A dead man in the grave cannot help. Christ rose and lives.)

D. "For whosoever shall call (pray in your heart for God's forgiveness) upon the name of the Lord shall be saved" Romans 10:13. PRAY AND TRUST HIM NOW.

SUMMARY OF THE ABOVE

Scripture instructs the unsaved to "believe" on the Lord Jesus. This means to fully surrender yourself to Him, in loving trust that He will save your soul and forgive your sins. The moment any person trusts or believes in Christ; that He died for their sins, (Step Two), and that He rose again and will call on Him to save them, He will do just that! At this point the new-birth is an instantaneous gift from God. It is ALL a miracle of God's saving grace.

IF YOU HAVE CAREFULLY OBEYED THE ABOVE AND TRUSTED CHRIST WHAT IS THE NEXT STEP?

Now that you have turned from your sins and by faith received Jesus, the Messiah, the Son of God as your personal Lord and Savior, read the following Bible verses.

John said: ". . . the blood of Jesus Christ His (God's) Son cleanseth us from all sin" I John 1:7. You are now clean from all sin. See also Hebrews 10:17.

Paul said: ". . . Christ also received us to the glory of God" Romans 15:7. Jesus Christ has now received you as His child and God is glorified. See Galatians 3:26.

Jesus said: ". . . rejoice, because your names are written in heaven" Luke 10:20. Imagine, your name is now written in heaven's book of life! See Revelation 20:15.

Please write to us about your new faith in Christ. We will send you information on how to continue in the Christian life. God will be with you for ever. Read His promise in Hebrews 13:5-6. And remember He said this to YOU! Now, live the rest of your life to the glory of God and fulfil your "vocare" to His everlasting honor. Try to remember that soon life's little day will be over. *Now* is the time to live for The Savior and tell others of his wonderful salvation.

When we have at last passed through this vale of tears, I will meet you in wonderful heaven and together we shall enjoy God for ever. This glorious prospect has been made ours through what Christ did on the cross in dying for our sins, his resurrection and ascension. Find a good *Bible living church* and work there to get the gospel that saved you to others. What an honor to live out our few days on earth to the praise and glory of the Lord Jesus Christ, God's wonderful Son. Amen!!!

****

Please note the mailing address below if you have questions and wish to correspond. If interested in extra copies of this book and a list of other titles by Missionary Henry R. Pike please write the following address.

Head To Heart
P.O. Box 25215
Greenville, South Carolina 29616
USA